FOUNDATIONS OF VISUAL COMMUNICATION

T0386436

Drawing upon theories from visual studies, critical visual culture studies, and cognitive psychology, and with a special focus on gender and ethnicity, this book gives students a theoretical foundation for future work as visual communicators.

The book takes a closer look at the interwoven character of perception and reception that is present in everyday visual encounters. Chapters present a wide variety of visual examples from art history, digital media, and the images we encounter and use in our daily lives. With the tools to understand how images and text make meaning, students are thus prepared to better communicate through visual media.

This book serves as a main or supplementary text for visual communication or visual culture courses.

Yvonne Eriksson is Professor in Information Design at Mälardalen University, Sweden.

Anette Göthlund is Professor in Visual Arts Education at Konstfack University of Arts, Crafts and Design, Sweden.

FOUNDATIONS OF VISUAL COMMUNICATION

How Visuals Appear in Daily Life

Yvonne Eriksson and Anette Göthlund

Routledge
Taylor & Francis Group

NEW YORK AND LONDON

Designed cover image: Hans Henningsson

First published 2023
by Routledge
605 Third Avenue, New York, NY 10158

and by Routledge
4 Park Square, Milton Park, Abingdon, Oxon, OX14 4RN

Routledge is an imprint of the Taylor & Francis Group, an informa business

Library of Congress Cataloging-in-Publication Data
Names: Eriksson, Yvonne, author. | Göthlund, Anette, 1965- author.
Title: Foundations of visual communication : how visuals appear in daily life / Yvonne Eriksson, Anette Göthlund.
Description: New York : Routledge, 2023. | Includes bibliographical references and index.
Identifiers: LCCN 2022060376 (print) | LCCN 2022060377 (ebook) | ISBN 9780367771553 (hardback) | ISBN 9780367769635 (paperback) | ISBN 9781003170037 (ebook)
Subjects: LCSH: Visual communication. | Visual communication--Methodology.
Classification: LCC P93.5 .E75 2023 (print) | LCC P93.5 (ebook) | DDC 302.23--dc23/eng/20230223
LC record available at https://lccn.loc.gov/2022060376
LC ebook record available at https://lccn.loc.gov/2022060377

ISBN: 978-0-367-77155-3 (hbk)
ISBN: 978-0-367-76963-5 (pbk)
ISBN: 978-1-003-17003-7 (ebk)

DOI: 10.4324/9781003170037

Typeset in Bembo
by SPi Technologies India Pvt Ltd (Straive)

CONTENTS

PREFACE

How do we interact with visuals? How do they interact with us, and with each other? This book takes a closer look at what happens between the actors involved in visual encounters. This includes a discussion on how we navigate our way through different visual landscapes and how we are guided by the visuals themselves. Visuals act and appear as instructions, entertainment, art, advertisements, and more.

We need to understand signs as symbols, as images and as representations. As in all kinds of communication, signs and symbols stand for something and we need access to the code in order to make sense of what we see. Also, what we *can* understand from a sign depends on our previous experiences, visual or otherwise. Our 'reading' of a sign is affected by the visual literacy we possess, and by the context and situation in which the encounter occurs.

The central theme of this book is to highlight the interwoven character of perception and reception that is present in every visual encounter. Each chapter uses a wide variety of visual examples to delve into the mobile, changeable and ambiguous lives of images —whether they appear as mental images or as physical items.

ACKNOWLEDGEMENTS

This project would not have been possible without the support from Mälardalen University and colleagues at the School of Innovation, Design and Engineering.

A special and warm thank you to our language editor Lisa Baumgartel.

We would also like to thank the artists Annika Elisabeth von Hausswolff and Peter Johansson for their permission to let us use their artwork and the family of Sten Didrik Bellander for letting us use the photograph in Chapter 3, which is part of a collection housed by Nordiska Museet in Stockholm; Photographer Kim Forchhammer and illustrator Håkan Ljung have kindly contributed to the book's visual material. Jonas Källberg made it possible for us to use one of his illustrations from the book *Svenska fåglar* (*Swedish birds*). Photographer Hans Henningsson and illustrator Lasse Frank, both at Mälardalen University, have provided both time and skills, which have considerably benefitted this book. We also thank Björn Westling, from Mälardalen University, and the Swedish Agency for Accessible Media for technical assistance and support. Anna Tellgren at Moderna Museet in Stockholm has assisted in contacts with the artists; thank you.

Finally, warm thanks to Agnes Silfverswärd for help with language checks and Judit Benedek for cooking and support.

INTRODUCTION

This is a book about visual communication. Therefore, it is also a book about visual culture. By extension, it is also about material culture, digital culture and other cultural 'forms'. After all, a visual is always materialised in some mode, technique or medium.

Communication, in any mode, is a *transformative process*. A performative act. Something happens, changes and is set in motion in a *communicative act*. Throughout this book, it is argued that this agency is inherent in both the visuals themselves and in the individual who is involved in the communicative act. Moreover, communication and representation can be understood as *social processes* of sign production, of *semiosis* (in Greek, *semaion* means sign). This means that people make meaning and communicate through different socially and culturally produced resources and modes, as described by social semioticians such as Hodge and Kress (1988), van Leeuwen (2005), Kress and van Leeuwen (2006). In our communication, we constantly combine or shift between spoken and written language and the use of images, gestures, colour and sound to convey what we want to express, and thus participate in the creation of the social world. Thus, to talk about multimodal communication might be more 'true to life'. However, since our focus here is on vision and visuality and the constant interplay between cognitive and socio-cultural processes while making meaning of the world we live in, we will mostly discuss visual communication and its relation to visual culture.

The visuals we will investigate in this book belong to different traditions, both the mundane and vernacular, as well as the scientific and extraordinary. They are created in different contexts and therefore also appear and act in different discourses. A picture can be used to portray things, illustrate relationships such as size and location, or stand in the place of an object, species or scenery as

DOI: 10.4324/9781003170037-1

a representation. However, a picture is always a representation, and is not the same as that which it represents. Therefore, a picture also exists under its own conditions.

Ultimately, this book is an attempt to make an extremely complicated subject more accessible. However, one book alone cannot unravel the complexities of visual communication. Instead, this book aims to raise awareness of these complexities and, therefore, also raises awareness about the necessity of learning how to decode and understand the visual messages that bombard us. Additionally, it seeks to raise awareness of the fact that we are all constantly involved in visual meaning-making and the production of visual messages. It is the authors' opinion we all need to improve when it comes to orientating ourselves in the visual landscapes we reside within and pass through on a daily basis, both as consumers and producers. Not least, this is something that should be taught in schools worldwide, and much more rigorously than it is done today.

What you will discover in this book

The ambition of this book is to elucidate the relationship between vision and visuality. That is, the perceptual conditions for our ability to see, and the socio-cultural aspect that guides us in the interpretation of what we see.

Chapter 1 begins by introducing and discussing what the authors call *visual landscapes*. That is, the complete surroundings we move about in during our everyday lives: everything from entire environments to the smallest details. These details can be distinctive or minimal, and require certain technologies such as microscopes to be visible to the human eye. However visual, they are also always material or materialised and have more or less tactile qualities. Visual landscapes appear differently in different parts of the world, as well as in different cultural contexts.

In the same way that a topographic and geographic environment transforms into a landscape in the eyes of the viewer, since any landscape is a sociocultural construction, the visual landscape is created through the act of looking. We frame what we see in front of us as *scenery*, as a view. When we then move about and orient ourselves in a visual landscape, we are constantly involved in visual communication, both with each other and with an abundance of visual signs and symbols—many of which we do not even register as 'visual communication' or as part of visual culture. This can include things such as road signs, information graphics and the like. All kinds of visual communication are necessary for our ability to orient ourselves. Thus, we are engaged in many types of visual environment mapping.

In Chapter 2, the discussion on visual encounters and everyday visual communication continues. One must understand communication as part of a system of representation. This is about how inner thoughts and mental images are exteriorised through sounds, words and gestures—and visual symbols. These are then combined into different kinds of visuals, such as paintings, photographs and pictograms. Another point of exploration is the skills we have developed in order to interpret and use visual messages, which can be defined as *visual literacy*. The chapter also discusses how the words we use to talk about visuals affect the meaning we derive from them.

What we see and how we perceive is not only a question of cultural tradition. It is also always about our ability to see. Therefore, we need to have some understanding of the perceptual and cognitive processes that are involved. For this reason, the authors of this book, as others before them, differentiate between *vision* and *visuality*.

How and what we see was already explained at the beginning of the 20th century by the so-called gestalt psychologists. Chapter 3 discusses the gestalt principles and how they affect the way we see, both from a more holistic perspective and in terms of how we combine single elements and thus turn them into meaning-bearing parts. In order to do so, we must understand what is characteristic of vision as well as visuality. What is important about visuals is not only their ability to depict and reproduce what exists in the visual environment, but also their ability to create mental images for us to act upon. This is, for example, how we come to desire certain fashion pieces or interior design objects.

To depict something that already exists is one thing, but to know how to produce images about a future we know nothing about, for example, is something else. This chapter explores examples of how this problem often leads to the reuse of 'old' symbols and visual tropes, only in another context. For a spectator to detect this, they need to be able to decode visual messages and ideas about the future—both specifically and in general.

However, visuals are more than representations. They are also agents. Chapter 4 focuses on agency: agency of the spectator and agency of the visual. In any visual event, what occurs can be understood as an encounter between agents; we do things with visuals and they do something with us. There is an ongoing and mutual influence between a spectator and a visual object. Important factors here include the impact of historical traditions as well as techniques and media. Some of the examples highlighted in this chapter show how historical norms and visual traditions are stronger than one might think—even if an analogue technique is replaced by digital media, those traditions remain visible.

Another characteristic of visuals is their ability to stir emotions and trigger memories. The way in which this is done depends on the context, situation and framing. We need to make a distinction between *context* and *situation*—something which is discussed in Chapter 5. One way to describe a context is to view it as an environment, framework or milieu. A situation, on the other hand, can be defined as a circumstance in a specific moment or a defined timespan when something is taking place or must be done. This distinction is also useful when it comes to understanding why we perceive visual messages differently depending on when and where we encounter them.

Even very simple symbols, like notations of different kinds, can require specific knowledge as well as previous experiences in order for one to make sense of them. When analysing and interpreting visuals, we need to *frame* their meaning. Framing is necessary in order to narrow down a context, and is something the spectator must do actively. The term framing has also been used by feminist scholars to describe the role of the female body in art history and how it has been controlled by both the artist and spectator.

The final chapter investigates how visuals, as physical objects, tend to travel across time and space. For example, an old city map of Amsterdam loses its original function once it is pinned to a wall for decorative purposes. Another kind of transformation occurs when a map is digitised and thus, transferred to a computerised form so it can be pulled up on one's mobile phone.

Mental images or pictures have the ability to move about. The same visual can appear in different contexts and media, and even simultaneously. Popular characters from children's books and works of art can be seen in picture books and museums, as well as on digital platforms or pieces of clothing, coffee mugs, notebooks, etcetera.

About the authors

Eriksson and Göthlund have been involved in visual studies, information design and art education for nearly three decades as researchers and professors. They bring together different perspectives on visual communication from different focus areas of interest. Yvonne Eriksson wrote her PhD thesis on the significance of pictures for people with blindness which involves tactile reading (Eriksson, 1998), and today, is a professor of information design. For her PhD thesis, Anette Göthlund studied the meaning of visuals in relation to everyday aesthetic practices and identity work among teenage girls (Göthlund, 1997), and is now a professor in visual arts education. A common ground for their research has always been that visuals of any kind do things both for us and with us—they have agency and they play an active role in what we remember and how, which is part of how we shape our understanding of the world we live in. The authors also agree on the idea that people, more or less consciously, use visuals and visual expressions of every kind in constantly ongoing communicative acts.

This book is made up of content Eriksson and Göthlund have been teaching to students in information design, and art education courses over the years. Some of it was previously presented in the first book they wrote together, *Visual Encounters* (*Möten med bilder* in Swedish) which was first published in 2004, followed by a second revised edition in 2012. However, they have since aimed to introduce new visuals and examples since this area is one of rapid change. Throughout this book, the examples chosen, as well as the way they argue for certain interpretations of them, all rest on the fact that their research and analyses are strongly rooted in an interdisciplinary way of thinking and doing.

This book is intended for students of visual studies, art history and visual design—or anyone who has a special interest in visual communication. Pictures and visual expressions can take ideas from anywhere in our surroundings and speak to us from everywhere. A deeper understanding of visual communication is a prerequisite for visual literacy which, in itself, is an essential ability to have if one is to navigate and take part in the world today.

1

VISUAL LANDSCAPES

How do we interact with visuals? How do they interact with us? And how do they interact with each other? In the following pages, we will discuss how we navigate our way through the visual landscape and how the visuals guide us.

Visual landscapes consist of visual representations such as drawings, photographs, paintings, digital models, sculptures, moving images and objects of various kinds; as well as architecture and cities. As a part of culture, visual landscapes are dynamic by nature, changing both over time and from place to place. The visual landscape of today is very diverse from the one that existed 200 years ago.

Changes in the visual landscape

The great quantities of visuals that exist today have a relatively short history. When the printing technique was developed in the late 19th century, pictures became commonplace in printed form, appearing in newspapers and books. For the first time in history, pictures were mass-produced, and the same picture could be spread over larger parts of western countries. This was the beginning of a more widespread visual culture which had commenced in the late 18th century for a more limited audience. From the beginning, illustrations in books and papers were taken seriously and, in educational textbooks, detailed descriptions of how to read and interpret the pictures were included (Eriksson, 2010). The interfaces students encountered in educational settings up until the mid-20th century were different kinds of visual representations such as planches, illustrated books, models and, later, diapositives and moving images such as Super8 and later VHS.

DOI: 10.4324/9781003170037-2

In parallel with the use of visuals in educational settings, access to the camera became affordable to people during the 1950s. Once Kodak introduced the Instamatic camera in 1963, it did not take long before not only adults but also children could get started with photography. The use of cameras among the general population turned people into co-creators of the visual culture to a larger extent than before. Photographs were collected in albums that were shown to family members and friends. Not only did people interact with the pictures, but the pictures also made them interact with each other regarding decisions on what to show and how to perform in front of the camera.

Even though the 'teenager' and a more defined youth culture started to appear during the 1950s, it was in the 1960s that—due to the emergence of a more affluent middle class—a culture for and by teenagers arose and contributed to visual culture. The walls of teenagers' rooms were covered with posters of movie stars and pop stars, sportsmen (and fewer) sportswomen. The agency of these pictures influenced how the young dressed and performed and who they identified with. Meanwhile, the walls of the adults' homes were more often adorned with framed but mass-produced prints of well-known works of art, or decorative pictures featuring flowers, nature, pretty women and the like. To have art on the walls was no longer a benefit for the few but became a possibility even for people with average incomes and an interest in interior decoration and art—albeit there was still a notable difference in the market as well as symbolic value.

Visual communication and its relationship to visual culture

As a starting point, it is important to take note of the relationship between *visual communication* and *visual culture*. Prerequisites for one another, visual communication and visual culture are necessarily intertwined. Since visual communication has to do with the interaction between visuals and the people observing them, it is, to a large extent, culturally bound. A common ground for this book is that visuals, of any kind, do things both *for* and *with* us. That is, visuals have agency; they play an active role in what and how we remember something, which is part of how we shape our understanding of the world we live in. Whether done consciously or not, we use visuals and visual expressions of every kind as part of constantly ongoing communicative acts—nothing is too insignificant to be considered part of one's daily visual communication. This means that we also step outside a merely observational mode to take a more active role in the interpretation of visuals.

Visual artefacts influence us in our daily lives, both at work and in our spare time. In a broad sense, everything in the environment belongs to visual culture. A picture belongs to visual culture. But visual culture can also stand for an idea, thought or object. To grasp the concept of visual culture, one must first understand that it is not the pictures or visual objects themselves that constitute the visual culture; rather, these should be viewed as its effects and products. At least since the Age of Enlightenment, all the thoughts and ideas that are the driving forces of visual culture are related to questions about vision, visuality and their connection to knowledge (Mirzoeff, 1999).

Visual culture is spatially organised, a characteristic which helps us to navigate it. When we navigate in space, the buildings and objects—such as the plants and trees arranged by landscape designers—help us find our way around. The ability to navigate is often attributed to eyesight; however, other bodily experiences are also involved. Therefore, one must talk in terms of modalities; the senses that are involved when navigating and orienting oneself in the environment. Such modalities were already known to the city planners of ancient times who, according to their belief that all senses should be stimulated, would consider the sound of rippling water as something important for inhabitants. In the examples discussed in this book, the point of departure is visual communication. Even if it is not immediately obvious, visuals always have something to tell us. An accompanying text, context or situation directs one's understanding and interpretation of a visual, as well as what one expects to see. Central to this book is the elucidation of how visuals create meaning and how they work as agents in different contexts and situations. The concept of visual communication will be explored further in the next chapter.

In the English language, a distinction is made between an *image* and a *picture*. A picture is a material object one can hang up on the wall, while an image is something that appears within a picture (Mitchell, 2015:16). An image appears in the memory (the *mental image*) and can also emerge verbally as a metaphor. Thus, there is a difference between the various kinds of pictures that are included in visual culture and the mental images they might produce or be a product of. Many people collect pictures as memories or souvenirs on their smartphones or computers, or in their photo albums or boxes. Some people systemise their pictures and categorise them into different folders, while others leave their collections unspecified. Pictures might fall out from a book where they were being used as a bookmark or randomly turn up on one's computer or phone. This can be compared to recollections of the past, where memories turn up as mental images. Recollections are shaped by our surroundings and previous experiences, by movies and pictures or by novels we have read. Such recollections are crucial not only for how we meet the environment or new milieus, but also for how we understand visual representations.

The meaning of 'culture' in visual culture

Visual communication is obviously conducted within—and to a large extent *with*—visual culture. What it requires of those participating in it is *visual literacy*. In short, visual literacy is the ability to decode visual messages. This concept will be expanded upon further in Chapter 2. There are also certain perception principles at play, which will be introduced in Chapter 3. But first: What does the 'culture' in visual culture mean?

Culture is, of course, a very complex concept in itself. It can refer to the fine arts, sometimes called a narrow or aesthetic understanding of culture. It can also refer to a broader, ethnographic view of culture: the culture that we all engage in and create through our everyday practises, including traditions, rituals, as well as the creation of art, literature and so on. Thus, there are local cultures as well as national, trans-national and global cultures. There are subcultures, countercultures as well as hegemonic cultures. Different cultures create different cultural expressions and develop their own traditions. For example, even though contemporary visual media (television, film, photography, drawings, etc.) are, to a great extent, globally transmitted and owned by global companies, the visual representations are often interpreted differently due to individual cultures and experiences (Eriksson & Fundin, 2018). Of course, there are also differences according to geographic and ethnic cultures, since different historical, geographical and ethnic traditions leave their imprint on visual culture. In other words, the global and local exist side by side, sometimes becoming 'glocal'. It is also important to recognise that other interfaces, such as organisational or company cultures, can actually override geographic or ethnic culture borders; for example, in certain professions or within global companies that have developed or instigated a strong 'company culture'. Another way of looking at this is to notice how one person often belongs to or acts within several 'cultures' at the same time. Even if an ethnicity is connected to a certain religion, language, nation or set of beliefs, it does not have to be synonymous with it—especially not today. A Swedish-born person can marry a British person with Indian ancestry, convert to Islam, and then move to India to work at an international company and become incorporated in that specific company culture. By learning to see through the layers filtering one's perception, it becomes possible to uncover norms, traditions, and alternative histories within the visual cultures one creates and lives in.

If with the help of visuals, it is possible to communicate globally and create a feeling of 'togetherness'—as in different fan cultures where members recognise each other wherever they go—visuals can also contribute to a feeling of exclusion and alienation. The alienation can be self-imposed, a distancing by a smaller or larger group which may lean on political, cultural or ideological arguments (or all of them together). Often, these groups are identified as subcultures or countercultures and express their affinity through certain styles or visual symbols.[1] In this manner, they also express differences from something or someone in particular. Among the initiated, such expressions also become visual communication. Although it may not take place in a conspicuous manner, it still performs the same act of distancing on the one hand and community building on the other. This kind of visual communication can also be found within the top level of society where, similarly, discrete elegance is a way to ensure that only the initiated get the message—only the connoisseur will notice if the Rolex on someone's wrist is real or fake.

Visual culture demonstrates a history of many groups being *made* invisible or strange and, by that means, they are ignored or identified as exotic. Due to the history of the Global North colonising the Global South, this has to a large extent positioned people from non-western parts of the world or minorities as 'the other'. Visual culture has, in that sense, played a part in producing and reproducing otherness as a way of distancing certain norms, values and ideals from one another. There are, however, several groups of people who have been assigned the position of 'other', 'different' or 'inferior'—or been more or less erased from the visual culture in different historical times, depending on the purpose. This also holds true for women and people with disabilities. The complexity of these acts can be understood if one applies an intersectional perspective that combines analyses of gender, class, ethnicity, ableism and ageism. It is important to notice and ask, 'who is looking at whom—and how, where, when and why?' As well as, 'who holds the power of looking?' (Sturken & Carthwright, 2002, see especially chapter 3). Critical visual culture studies offer such a theoretical framework.

Based on the above, it should be obvious that when talking about visual culture, one talks about it in the plural and must consider it as something that is produced, consumed and practised in a never-ending flow. A visual culture also *produces* and *acts* as visual communication.

Globalised visual culture and intercultural collaboration

Since communicating, both visually and otherwise, is facilitated by technical development and global communication systems on an ongoing basis, opportunities are increasing, but so are the challenges. Consider, for example, a company strategy that is meant to be operationalised in a global organisation. It must expend even more effort just figuring out how to communicate a strategy—especially considering the many cultural aspects a global company must take into account. One of the challenges is creating a common idea about a future goal; this can be defined as *a shared reference*. Not only do different experiences and knowledge bases influence the mental image of the future, but so do the many different cultures that strengthen the global presence of a company (Smith & Stewart, 2011). To create a shared understanding of the future, different strategies are used, such as visualising desired goals (Eriksson & Fundin, 2018). Since one cannot imagine something that is not yet known or of which one lacks previous experience, pictures of the future are necessarily related to the present. Therefore, a picture of a future state needs to be—or usually is—anchored in the present and with historical references. From a global perspective, such agreement on the present and the future is very diverse and highly dependent on the living conditions in different parts of the world. In rich and well-developed countries, the act of picturing the future mostly yields motifs featuring smart cities and high-tech solutions. Meanwhile, in less affluent African countries, for example, visuals of the future also include pictures of healthy children in school contexts, successfully cultivated crops and pictures that expose differences in living conditions and related aspirations and desires for a prosperous future.

In one study centred around an intercultural collaboration, visuals came to play a crucial role even though the national cultures and languages were different (Wlazlak et al., 2019). The study explored the role of visual representations in supporting communication between a research and design team and geographically distributed suppliers for a new product development project. It specifically focused on the design and use of visual representations as a feasible means of communication between the distributed actors when they encountered communication challenges originating from differences in English language skills as well as work experience. The project addressed different challenges that the different groups were experiencing related to various work processes, especially regarding how the work processes were visualised. One challenge was related to the improvement and correction of different product parts. The design team in Sweden was having difficulties communicating with the group in China due to language obstacles and a lack of experience reading CAD files. As a solution to this communication problem, the Swedish team created what they called 'picture books' (Figure 1.1).

To create these picture books the Swedish Research and Development team started to take photos of the delivered components that were not produced

FIGURE 1.1 Illustration from the project's picture book, cited from *Journal of Engineering Design*, 30(8/9).

This picture illustrates how the geographical distributed production team communicated through the use of visuals. Using photographs and CAD drawings to which they drew arrows with accompanying text boxes, the team was able to communicate about errors that needed to be addressed either through adjustments or larger changes. Illustration from the project's picture book.

according to specifications. The team also produced printouts featuring drawings of components to which annotations, including text and arrows, were added to explain what was produced incorrectly and what needed to be modified in the next series of components. The team then sent these to the suppliers and denoted all visual representations as picture books. According to the team, this became a simple but effective way to communicate with the suppliers. In other words, the picture books became an essential element of the devised communication procedure, where Chinese engineers were engaged in translating the text on the photos and printouts from English to Chinese. As a result, the suppliers started to implement the requested modifications, ultimately producing and delivering components that fulfilled the engineering change order. According to the Research and Development team, the introduction of the picture books became a key means of conveying the requested modifications (Wlazlak et al., 2019).

Conditions for interpretation and use of visuals

Visual communication has similarities to other kinds of communication, such as written and spoken language, but it is also different. For example, the way one speaks (in a calm or stressed tone of voice, for example) and reads a text aloud influences how the message is perceived. In the same manner, the reception of an original painting will change if it has been reproduced, and depending on what material it has been reproduced in as well as where it appears—even if the motif remains the same. The ontology of visuals is closely related to the epistemology of visual representations. For reference, ontology is the study of being or how one understands 'reality', and epistemology is the study of knowledge or what one considers to be 'knowledge'.

Questions that will be revisited throughout this book are: 'In what ways do visuals communicate in their different semblances and the different contexts and situations in which we encounter them?' And, 'what are the conditions for interpretation and use of visuals—in cognitive as well as socio-cultural aspects?'

The visual landscapes we inhabit or visit are constantly changing depending on the frequency of the visuals, access to visual media and techniques. Access to visuals is very much dependent upon the kind of 'visual infrastructure' in use. It may be museums or galleries, the internet, cellphones, street signs or advertisements, whether as wall murals or light advertising.

Obviously, the visual landscape is something that changes not only over time but also from country to country and even between regions and organisations. To decode a visual message, one must be familiar with the cultural context in which it is created—either the ethnic or organisational culture, as discussed above, or the local culture. It has been stressed that we are living in an era of globalisation and that the internet and different digital communication platforms are accessible globally. As the example above indicates, it is not enough to have access to internet and digital platforms; there are still challenges regarding communication, especially in relation to language obstacles. In addition, we are still very much influenced by our local cultures. There is often tension between local and global cultures. However, this can also be regarded as a fruitful dynamic that yields perspectives on both local and global cultures. Still, we cannot take for granted the fact that we are able to decode visual messages created in contexts that are unfamiliar to us, even though they appear familiar. Luckily, we can all learn how to read and understand visuals and their messages—visual literacy is an ability that must be learned, and it ought to be taught globally.

The authors of this book live and work in the northern hemisphere and have been brought up within a certain European visual tradition. Despite opportunities to travel worldwide and visit many different local visual landscapes, most of the examples in this book are taken from contexts the authors are familiar with. This does not mean that the theories and perspectives discussed, or the analyses made, cannot be used in other cultural contexts. For instance, the following examples, one from Cameroon and one from Sweden, show that the meaning of objects shifts over time and transfers between settings that are different from the original.

The Namji doll and a Dala horse

The story of the *Namji doll* was told by a salesman who was selling antiques in a gallery in Johannesburg, South Africa. He explained that the Cameroonian Namji doll is used by pregnant women to help them get used to carrying a child prior to giving birth (Figure 1.2). A more correct history, however, is that such

FIGURE 1.2   Namji doll.

Photography: Hans Henningsson.

dolls are expected to encourage fertility. But these dolls are also made for young girls to play with; they strap them to their backs and carry them around to mirror the responsibility of their mothers. Not unlike play with baby dolls performed by little girls all over the world. The dolls are also kept by women for good luck when trying to become pregnant or to help bring forth easy childbirth.

In Sweden, one will often come across colourful carved wooden horses, painted red and decorated with a distinctive pattern—called a *kurbits* pattern—in mainly yellow and green, or white and blue. According to the story about the tradition, it all started in the 18th century when forest workers, staying in timber huts in the villages around the small city of Mora in the Dalarna region, began to spend their evenings carving wooden horses. Much later, in the 1830s, the horses acquired their characteristic pumpkin pattern (*kurbits* comes from the Latin word *cucurbita*, which means pumpkin). They were sold in the villages and travelled with traders around Sweden. In 1939, the painted wooden horse from Mora became an international celebrity when it participated in the World Exhibition in New York. The Dala horse has been a symbol for Sweden in general—and for Mora in particular—ever since. For many people visiting Sweden, it is a must-have souvenir. However, the Dala horse is often bought from a Stockholm tourist shop, far from Mora and with no connection to its tradition. Today, one can also find the Dala horse in different materials—such as glass and metal—or without any colours and only the characteristic shape reproduced (Figure 1.3).

Collecting African masks and sculptures is a tradition that started in the early 20th century when they became an inspiration for Cubist artists such as Picasso. In many parts of Africa today, tourist shops and markets sell a mix of masks and dolls, among other items, as 'African'—rarely with their correct origin, function or usage mentioned. The interest in non-European objects has partly changed the European visual landscape but also the understanding of certain aesthetics. World Exhibitions and the idea of advertising different nations can be understood as an early form of 'nation branding' (Gienow-Hecht, 2019); thus an artefact with a strong national identity and aesthetic such as the Dala horse becomes

FIGURE 1.3 A traditional red Dala horse.

Photography: Hans Henningsson.

FIGURE 1.4 *How to Cook a Souvenir*, Peter Johansson, 1990–1992.

The artist Peter Johansson saws up Dala horses, packages them in traditional food wrappers, weighs the wrappers and then lays them out as if they were food.

Photography: Peter Johansson.

a perfect symbol for Sweden. But, just like the Namji doll from Cameroon, the Dala horse can also turn into a souvenir from a distant 'North', regardless of its local origin. The meaning and tradition that the Namji doll and the Dala horse once communicated are thus transformed not only once, but several times over the course of their existence.

As a comment on this way of reasoning, the Swedish artist Peter Johansson has played with national symbols of various kinds. Among them is a piece titled *How to Cook a Souvenir* (Figure 1.4). This artwork consists of the artist (mis-)treating the wooden horse as a consumer good—food—and it ends up as a sliced Dala horse wrapped in typical food packaging.

Navigating in a changing landscape

What we notice and what we pay attention to and really see in the visual land-scape depends on where we are moving about, what our focus and interests are, and what kind of previous knowledge we have, as well as on the situation. It's important to note that *looking* and *seeing* are not actually the same. Looking at something means that one directs one's eyes in order to see something, a physical movement. One must look before one can see. Seeing, on the other hand, is to perceive something. And to be able to make sense of what one sees, one must utilise previous knowledge and interpret the context one is in.

If, for example, one were to drive a car or ride a bicycle on a crowded street, one would have to be very focused and look at the traffic and the traffic signs to see and decipher the information about what rules and roles are expected from fellow road users. Here, the intention of the visual communication via the road signs is to inform road users about the traffic rules. If one walks along the street, one may pay less attention to the traffic signs and more attention to the signs telling the names of the streets, the signs of different shops and advertisements displayed in the surroundings.

How to navigate with help from visual input is something we learn over time. How we experience visual input and our ability to interpret it has also changed on a societal level. Most people can estimate the speed of a car when aiming to cross a street—something we were not trained to do a hundred years ago. We are also able to interpret complex animations and speed in moving pictures since we are exposed to these kinds of visuals in our everyday lives. This was not the case in the early years of motion pictures. For example, when comparing the rhythm and velocity in editing and scene changes of early cinema with, say the action movies of today, it becomes obvious that cinematic speed is also something we have learned to both perceive and understand (Corrigan, 2016; Virilio, 2012).

The emergence of the outer eye

A lot has happened in the visual landscape since the internet was first commercialised in the mid-1980s. We have witnessed a constantly growing number of personal computers, and when the internet became truly international, the number of internet hosts reached about 16 million (Cohen-Almagor, 2013). At that time, the internet was connected via telecommunication. From the beginning, it was not possible to send high-resolution pictures, and the internet was mainly used for text communication. In the year 2000, the first phone with a camera was launched and people grew increasingly interested in phone photography. It became possible to transmit pictures, and a culture of digital snapshots developed on a broader level. People began to take pictures and document their everyday lives, including what they ate, what they bought and where they spent their vacations (Wagner, 2011). Not least, people began to take pictures of themselves, aka selfies. Doing so was suddenly so much easier than using the self-timer of an analogue camera. In parallel with the advent of cellphone cameras, the small digital camera continued to develop and become easier to handle. What happened when people started using digital cameras is that the quality of the pictures could be evaluated at the same time as they were taken. If someone at a dinner party started to document the evening with their camera, the people portrayed immediately wanted to see how they looked in the picture, as a way to check their appearance. With that, all events started to have an outer eye—the digital camera—which prevented people from forgetting about their appearance. Even though photographs have always had the ability to be mimetic, to show what appears to be 'the truth' while being more or less staged or manipulated, digital pictures allow such staging and manipulation in a much more approachable manner. Snapshots from life with friends and families presented on digital platforms have become a way to showcase idealised pictures of events and to perform identities. New visual norms for how to appear have developed gradually and, in parallel with the digital photo technique, and new visual landscapes have been initiated. Being both behind and in front of the lens, we tend to look more at how we appear than at the motif itself. This practise of monitoring the visual self can also be seen as part of the Late Modern idea of the doable self or the Self as a reflexive project.[2] In addition, most people know it is possible to use digital software to modify one's appearance and reduce wrinkles and blemishes. The supply of filters one can add over one's face with a single click or touch of the screen is vast. However, digital technology not only focuses on the outside but it also gives us access to the interior of the body.

In the 1950s, ultrasound was invented for medical purposes. Today, getting an ultrasound scan is routine for most pregnant women, at least in western countries (Swedish Agency for Health Technology Assessment and Assessment of Social Services, 2018). The parents usually get a photo of the foetus to bring home. With that, the first picture of the child is taken, already before it has fully developed or even been born. At the same time, it also gives women access to the interior body—in this case, the womb. It is not only ultrasound in relation to pregnancy that has changed the way we perceive our bodies. The technique is also used in several medical diagnostic processes, as well as in the medical industry at large. Endoscopy and gastroscopy are other kinds of examinations that use a digital camera technique to give us access to the inside of the body. The artist Mona Hatoum used endoscopy and gastroscopy in the video installation *Corps étranger*, from 1994, where the video installation invites viewers on a journey through the artist's body. During the journey, we pass through the heart, lungs and vagina, among other bodily parts. The journey is accompanied by the regular beating of the heart and the breathing of the artist.[3]

Visual thinking and the body

One must be aware of the intricate relationship between seeing and knowing. The information in a visual exists, but it does not become meaningful until we interpret it and use it. With that, the formulated visual serves as an offering to the spectator, but it has no meaning until that meaning is recognised and named. Otherwise, it is not possible to communicate it. In other words, there is no knowledge in a visual until a spectator has created meaningful content through decoding what 'is there' (Belting, 2005; Sandström, 1995).

The essence of various kinds of visual representations is their ability to communicate differently depending on the context and situation, as well as on the recipient's ability to decode and interpret the message. The epistemological tradition the authors of this book partake in regards a visual representation as something that needs to be understood within socio-cultural contexts as well as from cognitive and perceptual aspects. When we access the world, we do so through the body, which includes the senses, the brain, and gravitation. When we explore visuals, such as pictures of various kinds, sculptures or moving images, it is always in relation to the body. One either sits in front of a computer screen, stands in or strolls through a museum, flips through a magazine or walks around a sculpture, maybe even touching it. How we talk about visuals is also related to space; for instance, 'look at the left-hand side of the picture and you will see…' or 'on the backside of the sculpture you will find…' Some people might have trouble navigating left and right. But even if they do not, to point or look left or right when asked to takes longer than pointing back and forth or up and down. This is because 'left' and 'right' are not connected to the bodily experience of gravitation but, rather, are concepts we have 'invented' in order to point out directions (Tversky, 2019).

Thus, visuals belong to the domain of spatiality. For one thing, they are spatially organised, in either two or three dimensions. The spatial organisation of thoughts is also a way to remember things, but it also supports the ability to recognise milieus or objects in a visual representation. We tend to accept a drawing or painting as a representation of an environment if the parts of the picture are organised in the same way as in physical reality (Langer, 1951). This makes even an essentially abstract representation recognisable to a spectator. For example, consider a map where abstract symbols are organised to match a specific topography. In such a way, it becomes possible to interpret and use the map in order to navigate or get an overview of a landscape or cityscape.

Since perception is not an isolated phenomenon, our topographical, geographical and cultural settings matter. Therefore, the physical features of a setting, where it is located, as well as how it fits into the cultural context all have an impact on what we are looking at, how we are looking at it and why. For example, what one expects from a landscape painting is influenced by the specific genre as well as whether one has previous experience of the specific topography that is represented. If one recognises the landscape and, perhaps, has experienced at least a similar environment, say a beach by the sea, one can often 'feel' what one is looking at. Over time, we have learned to accept a range of different ways of portraying landscapes. Still, it is not a unified expectation but depends on cultural background and familiarity with the genre and its conventions. In many cases, we primarily look for what we expect to see since these expectations influence our perception. It is hard for us to recognise things that we have not experienced previously, including certain visual representations. This means that a producer of various kinds of pictures follows the tradition based on an interplay of different factors, and the spectators expect to see according to these factors.

Today, much of the interaction between individuals belongs to the sphere of visual communication which takes place on digital platforms where people post their pictures and share experiences. Consequently, we often equate *interface* with *computer interface* and tend to forget about the interface that exists between individuals and objects in the physical space. Our view of interfaces has become narrowed to the interaction with digital tools such as computers, smartphones and tablets. At the same time, we talk about extended realities that we can access via augmented reality, virtual reality, and holograms (HoloLens). The extended reality is limited to visual experiences governed by remote controls, and the body is reduced to hand and finger movements—even though one experiences one's body moving through the virtual world one has visited through VR glasses. The interpretation of visuals is, to a large extent, related to spatial understanding and thinking; something that is highlighted, for example, in a VR experience. Thus, visual thinking and spatial thinking go hand in hand, and an interplay between cognitive and perceptual processes is required in order to perceive the world. How we perceive objects and pictures, as well as their details, depends on where they are located (Arnheim, 1969).

Visual studies and visual culture studies

As visuals of different kinds have become a growing part of our societies, a new field of academic research and scholarly interest has developed: *Visual studies*. Starting in the 1970s, a more holistic perspective was advocated for in the study of visual communication. In such a holistic perspective, focus is placed on how language and visuals act and interact with individuals depending on the verbal or visual expression, its content, and the recipient's sociocultural background. In the literature, this is described as the *linguistic turn* and the *pictorial turn*. The term linguistic turn refers to the role language plays in how we create and understand the world, including how language performs values and ideals, ethnicity and gender (Krippendorff, 2006; Rorty, 1967). The pictorial turn can be described as a growing interest in and understanding of how individuals and groups of people use and interact with visuals in their process of making sense of the world (Mitchell, 1994).

Visual studies have been a subject in various academic disciplines such as art history, ethnography, anthropology, sociology and media studies since the early 1990s. The role of visual studies or visual culture studies and their heritage varies depending on the discipline. In art history, visual studies are also a part of what has been described as New Art History, in which the old canon of art history is questioned, especially concerning gender and ethnicity.[4] There has also been a growing interest and need to include other visual representations in what was traditionally defined as 'fine art' in art history courses. Today, the inclusion of subjects such as textile art, ceramics, photography and art by non-western artists and women in the syllabus is a standard procedure in our universities—only 30 years ago, it was not.

Visual culture studies encompass theories and methods about the practises of looking, as it relates to technologies for making things and ideas visible and 'thinkable' (Sturken & Carthwright, 2002). It also examines visual communication and the different forms of knowledge that appear in and through visual culture and communication. From this perspective, *visuality* is studied as something which is socially and culturally constructed. That is to say that we learn to see in specific ways, according to the society and culture in which we live and are trained.

The authors of this book are well aware of the dissemination of new-materialist theories using the concept of *intra-action* to discuss how bodies or entities participate in action with each other. It is possible that the concept, which was originally introduced by Karen Barad, can also become valid within visual communication studies to replace *interaction* when we are trying to understand the activities that occur in a visual event. This depends on both the ontological as well as the epistemological status we want to attribute to the actors involved: the visual, the spectator and the medium/technique. In Barad's view, interaction necessitates pre-established bodies that participate in action with each other, while intra-action understands agency not as an inherent property of an individual or human to be exercised, but as a dynamism of forces (Barad, 2007). However, this expansion of visual communication theory goes beyond the aim of this book.

By now, the concept of visual culture has been used for several decades. Today, visual culture studies are often presented as 'critical' visual culture studies or, as in the latest edition of *The Visual Culture Reader* (2013), which is still edited by and with an introduction by Nicholas Mirzoeff: 'Critical visuality studies'. Visual culture is not a term used to point to the fact that, at least since the Enlightenment, we have been living in an era overflowing with visuals of all kinds. Instead, it points to the interrelatedness of seeing-knowing, the ocularcentrism of this time; that is, the privileging of vision over the other senses in western culture. This idea is not new; both Plato and Aristotle gave primacy to sight and associated it with reason. But it is important to notice that interpretation of the written word also relies on vision. More contemporary writings on the subject have been introduced by, for example, Martin Jay (1993). When Mirzoeff argues for critical visuality studies, he says that visual culture is neither attached to a specific medium nor object. In fact, it actively opposes visuality: 'By visuality, I do not intend something like "the social practise of vision." Rather, visuality is a specific technique of colonial and imperial practise, operating both at "home" and "abroad", by which power visualises History to itself' (2013:xxx). Thus, the element of power is always close at hand when using critical visual or visuality studies (see also Sturken & Carthwright, 2002, chapter 3).

Another point that should be made already here in this chapter is that visual culture should not be considered to be 'only visual'; as Paul Duncum writes (2004, 45(3): 254), there are no exclusively visual sites. In parallel with the acceptance and implementation of visual culture studies in the curricula of universities, there has been a growing field called 'material culture studies'. Stemming from archaeology and other disciplines occupied with objects and their materiality, it is now widely used in sociology, consumption studies, design, etcetera, and has become a research field in its own right. At the same time, the dichotomisation between visual and material culture should only be done for analytical purposes; the visual is always also material and vice versa. Even a digital image is dependent on materiality, such as a screen of some sort, to be visible. Paul Duncum stresses the interaction between different communicative modes: 'All cultural sites that involve imagery include various ratios of other communicative modes and many employ more than vision' (Ibid.). Therefore, it is also adequate to talk about *multiliteracy* when addressing the question of people's ability to 'read' and make sense of, as well as create 'texts' of any kind [Cope & Kalantzis, 2000].

The basic argument in this book is that the act of looking is a more intricate practise than one might think. The ability to see something is, firstly, a function of cognitive resources. The ability to see something as something is not only possible in relation to experiences within the outer world (i.e., society, culture), but also in relation to mental images, which are formed by previous experiences. However, the act of looking is also based on other modalities such as touch and hearing. We can recognise a material in a visual representation based on a previous tactile experience with the same material, which will affect our experience of what we look at.

Key chapter takeaways

- Visual landscapes consist of visual representations which are in a constant state of change.
- Visual communication and visual culture are prerequisites for one another and are necessarily intertwined.
- To decode a visual message, one must be familiar with the cultural context in which it was originally created.
- Since visuals have agency, visual culture plays a role in producing and re-producing norms, values and ideals. This is why we need to understand the processes of encoding and decoding visual messages.

Notes

1 One of the first to conduct research on this subject was the sociologist Dick Hebdige who, in 1979, published the influential book *Subculture: The Meaning of Style*, in which he looks into postwar Britain's youth subcultures and interprets their styles as symbolic forms of resistance.
2 One of the most well-known theorists on the subject of Late Modernity is sociologist Anthony Giddens. See, for example, *Modernity and Self-identity* (1991).
3 The video is available, for example, on YouTube.
4 See Jonathan Harris, *The New Art History. A Critical Introduction*, 2001.

2
VISUAL COMMUNICATION IN PRACTICE

Visual communication can be defined in various ways. It can be defined as face-to-face communication, where people interact with gestures and mimicry (Tversky, 2011). Or it can be defined as one or more visual representations, such as photographs, drawings, artworks, advertisements, movies and pictograms.

Even though we use it in different ways, visual communication is a part of every culture. Even a very simple symbol can carry complex meaning; something that needs to be learned. We use visual communication to express ourselves with the aim of sharing thoughts, ideas, emotions or information. Companies use visual communication to advertise products, and public organisations use it as a means of supporting citizens in their daily lives. For example, visual communication helps citizens find their way to the closest hospital or bus station, or it helps people identify where to park their car. We come across logos and emblems every day which represent everything from coffee shops and toilets to ATMs. Such visual communication helps us to identify things in our environment and navigate in the correct or intended direction.

Our use of visual communication can be conscious or unconscious, and is more or less a part of a tradition or norm. Consider the clothing we wear, for instance. A uniform can communicate a specific profession (e.g., a police officer, pilot, or doctor), a bathing suit can signal that one is headed for the beach, and a formal suit may indicate that one is performing office work. The field of visual communication takes into account everything that is visible—amounting to a broad spectrum to investigate.

DOI: 10.4324/9781003170037-3

Visual communication and representation

Regardless of whether the content is complex or not, all communication is an externalisation of our 'inner voice', our thoughts. The purpose of communication is to make such thoughts accessible to and understandable by someone else. Whether we wish to explain a concept, call attention to something, or entertain, communication is all about sharing with others. In fact, the etymology of communication is the Latin word *communicare*, which means to share, to make common. In order for this act of sharing to take place, there needs to be a *common language*—a cultural code, different kinds of signs—that has been agreed upon by the group of people partaking in it. It can be a cultural code that is agreed upon on a national level, or it can be one that is shared by a very small group or community. Some cultural codes are intended to include as many people as possible, while others are more exclusive in aim and are only shared with those who have been initiated.

Apart from a common code system, every communicative act is dependent on a medium, whether it is text, speech or a visual. Visual communication, in all its aspects, can also be considered to enact what Nicholas Mirzoeff (1999) calls a *visual event*: '...an interaction of the visual sign, the technology that enables and sustains that sign, and the viewer.' Mirzoeff also introduces the term *visual technology*, by which he means 'any form of apparatus designed either to be looked at or to enhance natural vision, from oil painting to television and the Internet' (1999:13). Such technology, then, also functions as medium.

Visual communication, or any communication for that matter, must be understood in terms of how it works as a system of representation. It is through the different languages we have access to that we create and exchange meaning, and produce and reproduce culture. We can only share and exchange meaning through a common language. The idea of a common language can be understood in different ways. It can refer to a common mother tongue or to a professional language which includes both verbal and visual representation. A common language can also consist of visual representations. For example, subcultures and global company cultures often develop and use a common visual language related to specific communication purposes to signal a common identity and ideals.

When studying visual communication, it is important to utilise different perspectives. From one perspective, we can study visual communication by exploring the intention behind what is being communicated and why. When doing so, it is crucial to remember that the meaning of visual artefacts changes over time and between contexts and, with that, the original intention loses meaning. This topic will be revisited later, especially in Chapters 5 and 6. Using another perspective, we can study visual communication by analysing the visual artefact itself, interpreting what it communicates as well as what is required to be able to interpret it.

In this book, visual communication is discussed from both perspectives. We start with the visual artefact itself and explore what effect it might have on the spectator. From that interpretation, a reasonable explanation regarding the intention behind what is being communicated can be offered. When these interpretations are offered, it is obviously the authors of this book who hold the position of the spectator. However, attention is also paid to instances when the spectator and receiver of a visual message is specific and targeted and to where they are expected to encounter the message.

Taking the spectator perspective into consideration means that we are dealing with both cognitive and perceptual aspects, as well as socio-cultural receptions and interpretations. Both are highly active processes. However, the cognitive and perceptual processes must be regarded as much more stable than the faster and more volatile process of reception. It is not only a matter of the recipients and their contexts; the question of *what* is represented and *how* it is represented in the visuals is equally important. This is because a representation can never be an exact copy or reflection of what it represents: each representation is also a construct in that it *re-presents* whatever it is pointing back to. A representation is something that appears and acts on behalf of something else and is therefore re-introduced. In this in-between moment, there are always alterations and shifts occurring. In this sense, representation is one of the significant practises that make up a culture.

A picture from a picture

Our smartphones are among the most frequently used communication technologies and media today. Perhaps more often than making phone calls, we use them to send and receive text messages, such as SMSs, and various visual messages, for instance MMSs, and to communicate via platforms like Instagram, Facebook, Snapchat, FaceTime or WhatsApp. Which platform is in use tends to change over time and with generations of users. These platforms are often used for text plus picture communication. An interesting feature is that when one types nouns or verbs, some smartphones automatically replace them with visual icons, so-called emojis. It is an automatic transformation from verbal to visual communication.

To be able to use visual communication and understand its meaning, it is necessary not only to analyse the content of a visual, but also to analyse how it is visually formulated and to evaluate what tradition it belongs to. The emoji is only one example of how we reuse visuals for the sake of communication. A tradition that can be traced back to pictograms; simple figures intended to be understood in a specific way.

Emojis

In 2007, Apple introduced the iPhone to the market and swiping and scrolling replaced the traditional button-pushing method of input. So-called smartphones quickly grew in popularity, especially among people who wanted to be part of the new digital era where communicating using visuals was 'the new'. In relation to smartphones, a frequent use of visuals means sending short messages using emojis. These very simple figures are mainly based on conventions, but we can understand some of them intuitively. The reason why we understand the meaning of emojis is because they are either isomorphic (i.e., high iconicity, they look alike) or their appearance is similar to traditional isotypes[1] or pictograms. The idea behind pictograms is that they should be standardised—there even exists an ISO 7001 standard (published by the International Organization for Standardization) for pictograms. Although the ambition is to create standardised pictograms that can work globally, there remains much variability in the way pictograms are designed, depending on the designer or cultural tradition (Figure 2.1).

While some emojis are more or less isomorphic, others serve as metaphors; for example, the heart and thumbs up emojis, or the one showing a green face indicating one feels sick or nauseous, or the '*zzz*' face which is a throwback to the tradition of comics and represents sleeping. Old metaphors and visual statements are transferred to and live on in new contexts and media. Things or phenomena that we experience as new often follow a well-established structure and tradition. The good thing about such traditional structures is that they make it easier for us to recognise and use visuals. This is because, in everyday life, we know how to interpret and use information that is already familiar to us.

Just as traditional pictograms undergo change, so do emojis—even more so in fact. Stemming from the original 'smiley-face', there is now an abundance of different symbols used for visual communication available both on our smartphones and computers (Figure 2.2). Work to keep the emojis updated is ongoing; including, for example, efforts to make them more inclusive by showing traits of different cultural or religious traditions. At the same time, many emojis are produced by global commercial companies, such as Apple and Samsung, and they appear globally as a result.

FIGURE 2.1 Photography: Yvonne Eriksson.

This image is an example of how ISO 7000 has been used to warn of slippery conditions. The simple symbol exploits our ability to intuitively perceive body language and our experience of what it means to slip.

FIGURE 2.2 Unicode Consortium, 2021.

The top 10 most frequently used emojis in 2021, according to research by the Unicode Consortium which they presented in the form of a word cloud.

Pictorial traditions

Other examples of visuals that show up on our smartphones are pictures that people upload on different platforms, often on a daily basis, showing everything from what food they are eating to their pets in funny situations, children and friends, or flowers and vegetables grown in their gardens. These photographs are rarely explained or commented on—but are often accompanied by a short, humorous or self-explanatory note—since a consensus regarding the aim and meaning of the motifs has developed over time. We can recognise the motifs of the pictures we encounter in family albums that follow the tradition of family and pet portraits, which goes back to the portrait paintings of at least the 18th century. We can also detect other pictorial traditions, such as Western still life paintings where food and flowers are arranged in ways that activate both sight and the other senses. References to cookbook pictures, pictures in gardening books, fashion magazines etcetera are also visible. None of this is surprising, since the visuals we produce always use previous pictures and visual traditions as models (Gombrich, 1960). When one looks at a cookbook, for instance, it is easy to detect different pictorial traditions; there are photos that emphasise the aesthetic qualities of the food itself and how it should be arranged. These photos often echo the still life paintings from the Dutch Golden Age. And then there are the cookbooks that are more or less similar to the glossy travel magazines and travel companions where food is presented in its cultural setting and tradition—often through a romanticised or exotic lens (Figure 2.3).

The way we use visual communication can be more or less explicit or intentional. For instance, supporters of a football team on their way to a game might

FIGURE 2.3 Illustrations of different kinds of cookbooks.

Photography: Hans Henningsson.

shout loudly and wear scarves, caps and t-shirts adorned with the team's name, colours and symbols—which help bystanders identify 'their' team. Sometimes, a team can be recognised from a combination of colours alone; at least by those who are familiar with what the colours symbolise. An example of a more subtle form of visual communication is a blue adhesive plaster. Traditionally, Western society has trained us to recognise white or beige plasters as being camouflaged to match skin colour, with the exception of the children's variety featuring cartoon figures, or the brightly coloured plaster a chef might wear to prevent it from disappearing in the stew they are making. Today, however, it is more common for shops to only offer coloured plasters, as a visual statement against labelling 'white' as skin colour.

Obviously, visuals can do a lot of things simultaneously. Every visual serves more than just an aesthetic or expressive function. Visual expressions carry social, political and cultural significance, embodying several different communicative dimensions. In other words, a picture also has extra-aesthetic features. Pictures have served 'socio-cultural basic functions' in every historical period, which also allows us to use pictures as historical source material. A common example of this is a wall painting or altarpiece in a church. From early medieval times to the late 18th century, the painting's function was to illustrate the sermon and provide guidance to churchgoers. It was not to be considered as art. Today, we regard these paintings not only as art, but also as a source of historical knowledge. Such paintings illustrate, among other things, which Hebrew-to-Latin translation of the Old Testament was used (Shapiro, 1996). On the other hand, we cannot look at an old painting in the same way as viewers did when it was originally painted since we will always look at it through the lens of today's pictures (Bal, 1985). Most tourists who visit the Sistine Chapel with paintings (1502–1512) by Michelangelo will recognise the section featuring *The Creation of Adam*; and not necessarily from books about the artist or the chapel, but from different kinds of advertisements. The opposite exists as well. Those who were already familiar with Michelangelo's *The Creation of Adam* (Figure 2.4) most likely understood the reference Nokia made to the painting back in the late 1990s when the telecommunications company launched their 'Connecting People!' cellphone advertisement (Figure 2.5). The slogan is already history, but it illustrates how visual references can and have been used in various kinds of advertisements. In a more recent example, this caricature of the football player Zlatan Ibrahimovic, from a Swedish daily newspaper, is placed in the position of Adam (Figure 2.6). From his elevated position in the sky, he comes to life through the microphone which is presented to him.

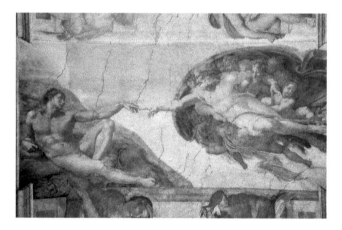

FIGURE 2.4 *The Creation of Adam*, Michelangelo, in late 15th century.

The Sistine Chapel, a papal chapel build in the Vatican 1477–1480. *The Creation of Adam* is one of the nine scenes from the Book of Genesis.

FIGURE 2.5 Advertisement for Nokia.

An advertisement for the telecommunications company Nokia from the late 1990s that paraphrased *The Creation of Adam*. The success of mobile phone manufacturers in the late 1990s and early 2000s has been attributed to this advertisement, in which the company focused on connecting people.

FIGURE 2.6   Illustration: Håkan Ljung.

The famous football player Zlatan Ibrahimovic has been portrayed in the position of Adam in this cartoon which appeared in a Swedish newspaper, Dagens Nyheter, published in May 2022, drawing attention to the fact that Zlatan is forty years old but still considered to be one of the best players in world.

Our mind shapes the world we see

It's not only socio-cultural aspects that matter in visual communication. We also need to consider the cognitive aspects. Our ability to imagine things influences the way we see and perceive the world, which ties into W.J.T. Mitchell's (2015) suggestion to distinguish images from pictures. This idea is also in line with The Nine Laws of Cognition.

The cognitive psychologist Barbara Tversky presents The Nine Laws of Cognition in her book, *Mind in Motion: How Action Shapes Thought* (2019). These laws serve as a basis for the discussions in this book, combined with socio-cultural perspectives. The laws are as follows:

There are no benefits without costs.
Action moulds perception.
Feeling comes first.
The mind can override perception
Cognition mirrors perception.
Spatial thinking is the foundation of abstract thought.
The mind fills in missing information.
When thought overflows the mind, the mind puts it into the world.
We organise stuff in the world the way we organise stuff in our minds.

These laws illustrate how the mind gets involved as we navigate the world and interpret our environment. Even though our mind and senses are dependent on physiological conditions, the way we think, the emotional condition we are in and how we organise 'stuff' in our mind is also highly dependent on the cultural traditions that we belong to, as well as on our living conditions. It is a relationship between cognitive aspects and a socio-cultural perspective, which is a combination of cultural traditions, norms, socio-economic conditions and societal aspects.

Figures 2.7–2.9 shows examples of three kinds of visual communication. Despite being very different, they all demonstrate the relationship between cognitive aspects and socio-cultural tradition and understanding.

The first picture was taken from a hotel in London, where a pictorial language is used that can be recognised from the movies, especially crime movies, where a dead body stored in a cold room is marked by a tag attached to the toe. Looking at the tag in the hotel, one might experience discomfort if one belongs to or takes part in the discourse around crime movies based on Western culture. However, if one is not familiar with how tags are used in other contexts besides hotels, one will probably not feel any discomfort at all. To understand the use of the tag, one must have previous experience with hotels and the act of hanging a tag on the outer door handle to signal cleaning staff not to enter the room.

The second picture shows a sign that belongs to a trash bin for dog excrement. The sign's meaning is obvious to most people living in countries where owners are expected to pick up after their dogs. But if we take a closer look at the picture, we notice that both the photograph and the pictogram above the trash bin contain several levels of both cognitive and socio-cultural processes which are involved in the interpretation. When interpreting the picture, the spectator must understand and accept that the dog in the pictogram is not a specific one. Because the mind can override perception, one is able to fill in the missing details and can arrive at the conclusion that the excrement should be picked up off the ground using the plastic bag that dog owners are supposed to bring with them. In addition, one must know that this behaviour is expected from all people who walk their dogs. As such, the aim of the photograph can be different depending on the context it appears in. The aim could be to show a smart design of a trash bin for plastic bags containing dog excrement or—in the case of this book—to provide an example of how visual communication works.

The third picture shows an example of so-called *conventional symbols*, like the ones we find on maps. Conventional symbols must be learned and are built upon general consensus. The orange line around the tree means that it is part of a nature trail, and the additional blue line indicates that the trail goes in a circle. The photograph illustrates a kind of sophisticated visual communication that is culturally based, but also accessible to anyone familiar with the convention of following symbols and reading a map for various parts of a natural trail. In this case, it is especially important since this specific trail consists of approximately 10,000 km divided into about 100 different routes.

FIGURE 2.7 'Do not disturb' sign for hotel door.

FIGURE 2.8 Trash bin for dog excrement.

FIGURE 2.9 Marked tree showing a hiking trail.

Photography: Yvonne Eriksson.

Visual literacy

When discussing the interpretation of pictures, it is also necessary to understand how pictures are 'read'. When one reads a picture, one is decoding, analysing and interpreting its overall meaning. It does not necessarily mean that one is interpreting the picture in a broader sense—that is, in terms of its socio-cultural context and historical tradition. Rather, it is more about the ability to understand how to use the information. It is therefore possible to divide the capability to understand and use visual information into at least two layers. Firstly, one can learn how to use traffic signs and the maps of public transportation systems, or how to find one's way around with a map, without any knowledge of the visual representations' tradition. Secondly, if one wants to understand the language of pictures on a deeper level, it is necessary to take a broader perspective into consideration. One must understand the context and set of circumstances in which the pictures have been developed. Here, we are dealing with different competencies which can be described as *visual literacy*.

The term *literacy* was originally used in relation to the ability to read and write. It has since expanded and is now widely used in different academic and non-academic contexts, not least in pedagogical and learning environments. It is also connected to democratic values and is, for example, defined by UNESCO as follows:

> Literacy is the ability to identify, understand, interpret, create, communicate and compute, using printed and written materials associated with varying contexts. Literacy involves a continuum of learning in enabling individuals to achieve their goals, to develop their knowledge and potential, and to participate fully in their community and wider society.
>
> (UNESCO, n.d)

According to the basic definition, visual literacy can be understood as the ability to read, write and create visual pictures.[2] Literacy can be divided into three different levels: the ability to understand something; the elementary ability to use a picture; and the ability to elaborate with pictures. *Visual communication literacy* means the ability to identify different elements in a picture in order to understand its meaning and be able to use or redesign it or use it in another context or situation for other purposes besides the original. The level of visual literacy required varies from profession to profession. At a museum of fine art, for instance, the guide needs to know and master the works of art according to motif, technique and epoch, while the conservator needs to possess a level of visual literacy that enables them to assess the condition of a painting or sculpture. In another example, engineering designers and product designers using 3D CAD models for communication need to master all three levels of visual literacy, while a salesman of the end product only needs to master the interpretation and be able to describe the product's visual representation.

Visual communication literacy

Here, we are combining communication with visual literacy and talking about how visual communication literacy can be understood. In this context, visual communication literacy is focused on the ability to analyse, interpret and use visuals for communication. In early communication theories, communication was regarded as a one-way process. That is, someone conveyed a message that was received by a recipient in the exact way the sender intended. Most renowned is the so-called Shannon–Weaver model of communication (Shannon & Weaver, 1949). Today, this is regarded as a unidirectional transmission model with a passive receiver. The communication research and, not least, the reception research of recent decades have strongly questioned this model. Instead, the co-creative role of the recipient (i.e., viewer, reader) in the communication process is being increasingly emphasised. The sender (i.e., artist, author) can never have complete control over what the message will look like once it reaches the recipient, that is the spectator. Nor can they have control over the previous conceptions that may affect the recipient's interpretation of the message. It is therefore possible to talk about different levels of visual communication literacy. Visual communication literacy embraces both the sender (the one who formulates the visual) and the receiver (the spectator who analyses, interprets and uses the visual message).

In order to understand and be aware of how visuals function as 'an act of speech' in our everyday lives, we need to develop visual communication literacy. Almost every single visual representation is part of a dialogue with other visuals—both previous (historical) and contemporary visuals from different genres—as well as with the viewer. Such visual dialogues are 'invisible' if one does not recognise the references that are being made. But by developing visual communication literacy, it is possible to decode the ongoing dialogues and, in such a way, uncover the invisible structures that generate stereotypical visualisations such as gender, ethnicity, class and sexuality. Such visual dialogues can be understood as the way different visual genres interact, and are then referred to as *intertextual references*, or *intertextuality*.

Both the vocabulary and the pictures we use are thus representations of thoughts and values. But they are also co-creators of these conceptions, pictures and values. Having awareness of the necessity of a 'proper' vocabulary while speaking about something is often more common than having awareness of the values a picture 'speaks of' or represents. In the case of some pictures, it is obvious that they are not *come il faut* since they represent values that are not in line with contemporary understandings; for example, pictures with racist content. Meanwhile, other, less obvious values, are used unconsciously or unintentionally. Gender stereotypes are an example of values that tend to slip through more easily.

Lost meanings

If a picture and its contents are not read carefully enough or interpreted within the intended context, confusion often results regarding their meaning and intent. Or they are obscured by the fact that the original intended meaning of the visual message has changed over time, becoming obsolete.

These visual examples, originating from Sweden, are more or less incomprehensible to modern-day Swedes. The first, showing an upset gentleman pointing toward a glass and a bottle containing schnapps (a traditional alcoholic beverage), and a crawfish, says, 'NO! Crawfish demand these beverages'. This picture (Figure 2.10) can sometimes be found on kitchen walls, as a decoration, but very few understand the historical facts behind it. The strong Swedish tradition of eating crawfish in late summer, and accompanying the meal with beer and schnapps, is only part of the message. These pictures were part of a 1922 campaign connected to a referendum where Swedish people were given the opportunity to vote either for or against a total prohibition of alcohol. This was during an era when several countries were in a 'war' against alcohol and excessive drinking, not least within the working class. So, while the group advocating to

FIGURE 2.10 By Albert Engström, 1922.

Translation from Swedish: 'Crayfish require these beverages! You must refrain from crayfish if you do not vote NO on the 27 August'

vote 'NO!', against prohibition, leaned on arguments such as each man's right to decide for himself and holding on to tradition, the 'YES' side used other arguments (Figure 2.11). This was the first referendum in which Swedish women were allowed to vote, and while the 'NO' side used male voices to advocate a no (like in the crawfish example), the 'YES' side was supported by the strong sobriety movement and many arguments were directed toward women of the working class. An important argument used by friends of sobriety was that poverty was exacerbated by the fact that grain and potatoes were used to make beer and spirits and that some workers received part of their wages in spirits. All in all, they made a point of the fact that men drinking strongly affected the wives and children. This is the message one can read on the other poster: 'Payment day. VOTE YES!'

Visual communication involves a visual scenery that contains many different layers of not only traditions, conventions, and ideologies, but also *ontology* (how we understand reality) and *epistemology* (how we understand knowledge). On one level, visual communication is easy to understand since pictures can be recognised intuitively (which is not the same as understanding their content on

FIGURE 2.11 Artist unknown, 1922.

Translation from Swedish: 'Payment day Vote Yes!' The man has obviously received part of his salary in liquor, arriving home drunk the same evening to his distraught wife.

a deeper level). Pictures can be easily copied by another artist or producer—now more effortlessly than ever thanks to new technology—as well as imitated by the viewer. For example, one can imitate what is shown in the pictures of a glossy magazine containing advertisements and articles about how to dress for various occasions or how to design one's home. Often, in our consumption-driven economy, this is also the whole idea behind visuals. However, what is not necessarily obvious in a picture found in a glossy magazine is the value or ideology which is embedded in the style of the clothing, furniture or textiles displayed.

Visual perception

To be able to see something, eye movement is necessary. As a spectator, it is not enough to be aware and engaged, actively looking at what is in front of one's eyes. Rather, the ability to see is an interaction that takes place between the physiology of the eyes and the environmental conditions. We perceive and understand our surroundings through our senses. Some researchers believe that the ability to interpret the impressions we gain through our senses is innate, while others believe that we learn through experience to interpret the different sensory impressions we pick up through vision, hearing and touch. Most likely, the ability is innate, but the possibility lies in the culture—we learn through experience.

According to James J. Gibson, the ability to perceive through one's senses is innate. One learns to perceive and interpret certain signs through experience, and according to one's needs and the *affordance* of the sign or object. With the concept of affordance, Gibson was referring to the potential uses of any given object. What one sees as a potential use is connected to the observable properties of the object, but also to the need and interest of the observer. In *The Ecological Approach to Visual Perception* (1979), Gibson describes how one's ability to interpret different sensory impressions is adapted to the environment in which one lives. Gibson bases his ideas on the ecology of wildlife and describes the long evolution of the species as a reciprocal link between biological structures and their special environment. Gibson believes that the task of the senses is to capture information, and he calls them *perceptual systems*. The *orientation system* is fundamental to the other perceptual systems which are visual, auditory, haptic and taste-smell. The basic orientation system interacts with the other systems and serves as a frame of reference. If one follows Gibson's theories on ecological adaptation, it can be assumed that people who are visually active will be more skilled in interpreting and using visual information.

When we perceive our environment, we are not always aware of the continuous flow of visual and tactile interactions, nor are we always aware of the fact that our ability to perceive and interpret certain visual impressions is dependent on tactile experiences. When we look at an artefact, whether it is an object or a painting, our knowledge of it is based on nerve activities initiated by the light that is reflected from its surface. This light, which is purely physical in nature, reaches the retina of the eye where it is then transformed into a nerve activity that is transmitted to the brain. The vision is completed through both the visual stimulation of the eye and the interpretation of the visual—the stimulus—by the brain. To be able to see the world, first of all, physical energy is required: without electromagnetic energy oscillations there would be nothing to perceive, nothing to see and nothing to understand. In the brain, there are multiple connections between incoming signals and an abundant number of nerve units that give the visual objects meaning. The basic information is obtained from the eye and then organised by the brain into meaningful patterns. It is during this step that immense knowledge of the world, in general, is added to the sensory information: the object is interpreted (Solso, 1994).

Compared to insects, for example, the human eye is far from the most complex optical system. This is because, for humans, the interpretation of a visual perception takes place in the brain. Insects, on the other hand, merely recognise objects visually. Because the human field of vision is limited, we must constantly move our eyes to be able to clearly perceive entire surfaces. As a consequence of these eye movements, we can never see the whole picture at once. Instead, our view is based on the fact that we are looking at one small part in time which is added to a whole picture in the brain.

The active eye

In *Cognition and the Visual Arts* (1994), the American psychologist Robert L. Solso summarises the visual process as follows. Visual information is detected in the environment by the eye (step 1), is transferred into nerve energy, and then passes through the visual cortex's visual centres where the information begins its process in the form of simple surfaces and shapes (step 2). The visual signals are identified as contours, horizontal and vertical lines, curved lines and angles. These basic forms are combined into larger units and establish the basis for larger scenes (step 3). The semantic process is also part of this third step; that is, how one interprets the meaning or significance of what one is looking at. How we interpret what we see depends on our past experience and knowledge, and the same process occurs if we gain information from touch.

When looking at a picture, we distinguish its different parts by the contour lines of the depicted objects which creates a distinct shape against the background. The contours allow us to distinguish the different objects from one another. An outline appears in the boundary between two surfaces. Most commonly, contours in pictures are created by lines. These are also the contours we are looking for to be able to distinguish objects in our environment, not least in nature. It is through the contours that we discover shapes and can thus orient ourselves. If it is foggy or dark, for example, one cannot find these contours

(a)   (b)

FIGURE 2.12 The same foggy landscape in both photographs. It is very difficult, even impossible, to find one's way through a foggy landscape without visible landmarks.

The same foggy landscape in both photographs. It is very difficult, even to find one's way through a foggy landscape without visible landmarks.

Photography: Yvonne Eriksson.

and will therefore have difficulties recognising one's surroundings and finding the right path, particularly if one is to navigate based on sight alone (Figure 2.12a and b).

Cheating the eye

The reason we perceive lines so easily is that our brain is prepared to read these signals. So, here we can see that the condition of the eyes and the environment are interdependent and, with that, create the basis for our ability to perceive the environment visually. When we read a tactile picture using our fingertips, the same part of the brain is activated as when we look at a picture.

It has long been a desire of visual artists to create an illusion of reality. In the history of art, it is possible to identify several periods where artists have developed techniques that focus on *trompe l'oeil*, which can be translated to 'deceive the eye' or 'optical illusion', including the renaissance invention of the *central perspective* to create the illusion of distance and depth in paintings. But the impression of closeness and presence has also been sought after. In the late 19th century, so-called *realism* was based on creating a sense of presence by arranging motifs on the canvas in a way that gave the viewer the feeling of being a part of the event. This super-reality, as well as how to elaborate with colours and shapes to make the things portrayed look more 'real', is something we have come to see more frequently over the last decades with the advent of virtual art and virtual image making, for example in computer games.

The ideal of *mimesis* has had a strong influence on Western art through the ages. Plato spoke himself of mimesis, derived from the Greek word for imitation, as the re-presentation of nature. An interest in creating illusions in art is also noticeable in contemporary virtual art (Grau, 2003). It is quite easy to betray the viewer by taking advantage of how visual perception works. There are several explanations for this. One is how colours work in combination with one another. By using colours that have an impact on each other, it is possible to create volume. This is because some colours tend to 'pop out' from a surface, while others 'draw back' in relation to it. There are also other ways to elaborate with colours to create various visual effects. For instance, in the late 19th century, there was a great interest in how colour works in relation to visual perception. This can be observed in art, where the so-called *pointillists* developed the technique of applying very small, distinct dots of colour in patterns to form an image. When looked upon closely, the spectator's eye cannot identify anything distinct on the canvas. However, from a distance, the dots blend together visually and create form and depth.

One explanation behind the ability to cheat the eye is the limitation of visual perception. When viewing a visual artefact, it is impossible to focus on the foreground and background at the same time, or on two sides of a line simultaneously (Figure 2.13). Already in 1914, Edgar Rubin concluded that which side of a line one focuses on influences what one sees.[3]

FIGURE 2.13 Figure–ground.

What do you see? This well-known figure–ground picture illustrates that it is impossible to look at foreground and background simultaneously.

Attracting the eye

Producers of visuals want to draw attention to either a visual story they wish to tell, instructional information about how one should move about, or a specific element that will attract a potential buyer. There are, of course, several ways to attract visual attention. One way is to use the pop-out effect or to show something unexpected or crazy. Today, many companies leverage the effect of the unexpected. The reason why producers tend to use effects and elaborate with unexpected details in a visualisation is that, in general, people tend to look without seeing it seeing. Noticing what is in front of oneself is not the same thing as it.

Regardless of the original intention behind a visual artefact, by looking at it we are also able to simply enjoy and experience pleasure. In addition to art, even advertisements, technical drawings or maps can arouse positive feelings. However, the pleasure of looking has been considered taboo in several contexts, since looking is an act that cannot be controlled from the outside. The pleasure of looking is often a process that takes place inside a person and cannot always be formulated or expressed in a conversation. Therefore, the act is 'hidden' and inaccessible.

One might wonder why it is important to look, and why it is not enough to simply notice and register the contents of one's surroundings. Many people argue that they are not visually skilled and that they do not find it interesting to pay attention to visuals. With all respect to these people, the authors of this book argue that visual communication is crucial for all kinds of communication and highly influences the relationship between individuals and groups of people. But again: visual communication literacy is something that must be learned and practised.

Vision and visuality

The relationship between vision—the physical ability to see—and visuality—which is the ability to make sense of what we are looking at—elucidates the interwoven relationship between visual perception and visual culture. Culture influences visual perception, and vice versa. Hal Foster has described this in the following way:

> Although vision suggests sight as a physical operation, and visuality sight as social fact, the two are not opposed as nature to culture: vision is social and historical too, and visuality involves the body and the psyche. Yet neither are they identical: here, the difference between the terms signals a difference within the visual—between the mechanism of sight and its historical techniques /.../

> *(Foster, 1988: ix)*

Even if the viewing conditions are perfect, we do not automatically understand what we are looking at. For instance, when encountering Christian religious symbols, if one is not familiar with the Christian tradition, one will only see a man hanging on a cross and not identify him as Jesus. Likewise, if one is unfamiliar with Hinduism, one will fail to recognise the three principal gods: Brahma, Vishnu and Shiva. These examples are obvious, to some degree, while others are more subtle, even if they rest on cultural conventions and traditions. The most basic visual communication is also layered with cultural meaning, such as pictograms. Another example is how the different countries organising the Olympic Games develop their individual pictograms as a way of expressing cultural identity. In Figure 2.14, for example, it is possible to recognise lines of ancient Chinese seal signs printed on the mugs produced for the 2008 Games. Still, in addition to their traditional context, these sports pictograms must function as an internationally understandable representation of each respective sport.

The aim of the pictogram shown in Figure 2.15, for instance, is to help people with cognitive disabilities understand information about the Covid-19 pandemic. In this pictogram, it is to some extent, easy to identify the motifs. However, the meaning and aim of the pictures are not obvious. For this reason, every single picture is accompanied by a text, explaining what the picture represents. But still, it is hard to understand the intention of some of the pictograms. On the other hand, the partly vague meanings of the pictograms make it possible for relatives and caregivers to use them in a way that best suits the individual with cognitive disabilities. This pictogram illustrates the difference between recognising an object or scene in a picture and understanding its aim.

FIGURE 2.14 Photography: Hans Henningsson Pictograms designed by Hang Hai and Wang Jie.

A mug produced for the Olympic Games in China 2008. Pictograms designed by Hang Hai and Wang Jie.

Pictogram.se © Specialpedagogiska skolmyndigheten   The document can be downloaded at www.pictogram.se

FIGURE 2.15 Picture: SPSM/The National Agency for Special Needs Education and Schools.

Key chapter takeaways

- In all visual communication there is a relationship between perception, cognitive aspects and socio-cultural traditions and understandings.
- Visual communication is a practice that always requires visual literacy. This is something we can and must learn.
- It is through the different languages we have access to that we create and exchange meaning, and produce and reproduce culture.

Notes

1 An isotype is a drawing, diagram or other symbol that represents a specific quantity of or other fact about the thing depicted.
2 The term was first coined in 1969 by John Debes. Debes was the founder of the International Visual Literacy Association and, for several years, served as the coordinator of visual learning for Eastman Kodak Company. See the website of the International Visual Literacy Association, https://visualliteracytoday.org/
3 See Edgar Rubin's dissertation from 1915 *Synsoplevede Figurer* (Gyldendal 1915).

3

ANALYSING AND INTERPRETING VISUALS

In this chapter, we will delve into Gestalt Theory. Already established by the late 19th century, in recent decades, the theory has been updated—not least within the contexts of virtual reality, artificial intelligence and picture recognition. Gestalt Theory draws attention to how we humans automatically search for patterns in order to make meaning of what appears in the visual field. To take the next step—and turn patterns into something we can understand—we combine different visual elements into larger meaning-bearing units, and thus lay the foundation for an interpretive act to occur. We will illustrate this further in the following pages.

We will also take a closer look at the process of interpreting visuals. During the act of interpretation, the content of a visual artefact must be *conceptualised*, whether through speaking our thoughts aloud or simply thinking them. A visual's ability to make inner thoughts and ideas tangible, as well as to resemble something, are among its distinguishing characteristics. This *mimetic* quality is what enables people to follow visual instructions—whether they are in the form of user manuals, fashion or interior design.

The role of Gestalt Theory in relation to visual interpretation

While it is true that culture influences what we see and how we see it, it is also necessary to consider other fundamental aspects, such as eyesight itself. Historically, there has been great philosophical interest in seeing and visual perception. As previously mentioned, vision requires an active process. According to Aristotle (350 BC), 'The soul never thinks without an image'. The influential perceptual psychologist Rudolf Arnheim (1969) also argued that perception is equal to visual thinking. He regarded sight as an active process that takes place in the interaction between what we see and how we interpret what we see.

DOI: 10.4324/9781003170037-4

In turn, regarding sight as an interaction between what we see and our interpretation of it has consequences when it comes to how we perceive. Our thoughts are influenced by what we see and our sight is affected by our thoughts. That is, we see what we think and we think what we see. Therefore, one can argue that our thoughts are largely structured based on the visual impulses we receive, with the visual impulses from visuals making up an extensive part.

Arnheim defines sight and hearing as intelligent senses with which we think. We can think in shapes, colours, movements, and sounds. These elements are controllable and thus possible to define. They are also organised in time and space. To perceive something with the help of sight, a number of conditions must be fulfilled. It is not only the relationship between the different physiological properties of the eye that enables us to see, but also the brain's ability to interpret the impulses that come from the eye and also the circumstances under which we view an object or image. And, of course, there's the fundamental prerequisite to being able to see anything at all: light. How much light is required to perceive a given object or visual depends on the requirements for being able to distinguish its colours. In turn, light influences which colours we can perceive.

Even though many theories about vision and visuality have been developed over the last decades, and in relation to perception, cognition and socio-cultural aspects, Gestalt Theory is still relevant and utilised today by graphic designers, for example.[1]

The *Gestalt principles* were formulated in the early 20th century and should be regarded as a foundation for a system of how we perceive various *Gestalts*. (The German term *Gestalt* means form or configuration.) Several theorists were involved in the formulation of the Gestalt principles. As early as 1923, the principles that have given us a holistic view of how perception works were formulated by the psychologist Max Wertheimer. Wertheimer collaborated with Wolfgang Köhler and Kurt Koffka, the founders of so-called *Gestalt Psychology*. Some of the more fundamental Gestalt principles are referred to as 'The seven Gestalt principles of visual perception' and they will be discussed below. These comprise:

- Continuity
- Figure-ground
- Proximity
- Common region
- Similarity
- Closure
- Focal point

Research has shown that our ability to interpret something according to the principles of form is innate (Gibson, 1950; Hochberg, 1962; Ware, 2012). At the same time, it is important to point out that knowledge, environmental impact and training also affect our overall view and the meaning we make out of the forms our sight detects.

The Australian philosopher D. M. Armstrong has formulated a theory about how human concepts are structured (Armstrong, 1978). His theory is useful in discussions about similarities in relation to artefacts. Armstrong distinguishes between different domains. Spatial concepts belong to one domain, colour concepts to another, sounds to a third, and so on. In cognitive science, it is necessary to separate the information that is to be represented into different domains. Analogous to the discussion about concepts within cognitive science, the distinction between domains is useful when defining different kinds of models and their ability to represent actual objects (Eriksson & Florin, 2011). Armstrong's theory explains how we organise our perception based on already known phenomena and objects. For example, if a child is familiar with the fruit apple they will recognise an unknown fruit (for them) with the same shape, for example an orange, as yet another apple since the fruits share the property of roundness and, by that, belong to the same domain. Moreover, roundness is the higher order of the domains and thus overrules the fact that the apple is red (or green) and the orange is yellow-ish.

The law of the good curve and continuity

The law of the good curve aims to describe how the curve dominates when a circular shape crosses an angular one. Instead of perceiving the square and the circle as part of a single unit, for example, one perceives that the circle is positioned in front of the square. This is a visual formula that is often used in abstract modernist art.

Another of the principles formulated is the one related to the ability to perceive continuity. The explanation for why we perceive continuity is that an arrangement of objects (whether similar or different) with the same distance between them is interpreted as being continuous. But the way we perceive continuity can also be more like a process—like a series of pictures or a comic strip. To comprehend something as being continuous, some recognisable elements need to be represented from one frame to the next (Figures 3.1, 3.2).

FIGURE 3.1 Illustration: Lasse Frank.

The law of the good curve. This illustration shows two examples, the first of which is the law of the good curve which says that we perceive the curve as lying on top of the rectangle. In the second example, the dots are perceived as a line since they are presented as a continuum. The dimension in scale makes the line disappear in the horizon.

FIGURE 3.2 Illustration: Lasse Frank.

We read a series of images differently from written text. This is because image storytelling works with a different logic from spoken and written language. In the picture series, we see a woman jogging through the woods, but we also see a mobile phone in the foreground of the first frame of the series. An enlarged image of the woman's face with a clear direction of her gaze shows that she sees the mobile phone. We see her bend down and pick up the mobile phone in the lower left frame. In the transition to the next frame, the frame is broken and we see the mobile phone in the foreground and how the woman, now a half-figure, turns around when she hears a knock. This series is an example of how a cartoonist can work with different frame sizes and gaze directions to create a narrative.

Figure-ground

The fact that we cannot focus simultaneously on the foreground and the background of a visual is due to the characteristics of lines. That is, a line has two sides: A characteristic that has been noticed in the psychology of perception. In the case of line drawings, the two sides of a line can have consequences when it comes to how the picture is read. The most famous example is the figure

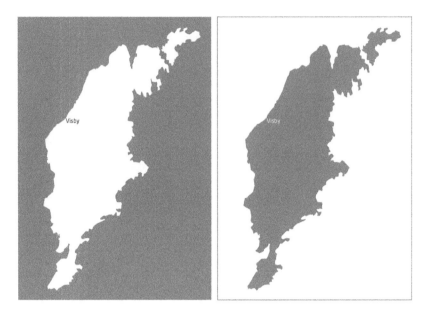

FIGURE 3.3   Illustration: Lasse Frank.

This map showing the Swedish island of Gotland is an example of what happens when we focus either on the blank surface or the dark one. As we are used to seeing land masses portrayed in a shade darker than the surrounding water, we may perceive the map on the right as a landmass with a lake instead of as a sea with an island.

where one can perceive both a vase and two profiles, depending on where one focuses one's gaze (see previous chapter). The same phenomenon occurs when one looks at a line-drawn map; one can either focus on the landmass or the surrounding water (Figure 3.3).

Proximity

When we look at a picture of a group of people or objects, our automatic interpretation is that the people or objects that are situated close to one another belong together. However, close proximity alone is not sufficient to make an accurate interpretation. For instance, although two cars that have collided in a head-on crash are close to each other, one does not interpret them as belonging together. The same applies to a picture of two individuals in a fight. The proximity law should therefore also be linked to other aspects that are primarily related to our previous experience, and this includes body language (Figure 3.4).

Common region

There are many indications that we perceive body language equally regardless of cultural background—even when looking at simple stick figures. This means that

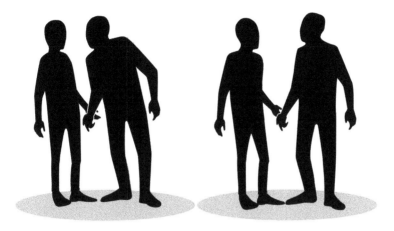

FIGURE 3.4   Illustration: Lasse Frank.

Threats and proximity. With very small changes made to a drawing showing different forms of body language, we perceive what can be described as closeness differently. In the picture on the left, closeness is threatening as the body language is tense, while the picture on the right depicts a kind of closeness that is not perceived as unpleasant.

we can read from an image if someone is threateningly close to another individual or if it is a closeness that indicates belonging. If things are grouped together by a border, they are also perceived as belonging together—what can be defined as a *common region*. The colours or shapes of the objects may not necessarily be the same but, by framing them with a line, they will be interpreted as being grouped together.

Similarity

Objects that look similar in a picture, or a field of view, tend to be perceived as belonging to each other or as more uniform than they actually are or need to be. For example, in a picture showing a group of squares and one triangular shape, the triangular shape will be perceived as being deviant from the squares, even though the square shapes are very different. On the other hand, a rectangle among a group of squares will be perceived as anomalous. Thus, it is possible to claim that the perception of deviance is relative (Figure 3.5).

Closure

As an example of closure, which means the illusion of seeing an incomplete stimulus as if it were whole, we tend to fill in what is missing. In doing so, we create a complete outline that gives a solid shape. A classic example of this is a drawing representing a human being where part of the outline is missing. Figure 3.3 shows an example based on a twenty-year-old advertising image for LU biscuits. The advertisement asks us to eat the low-calorie biscuits even if we are in good shape, as they are said to be both tasty and low-calorie. 'Eat a biscuit that

FIGURE 3.5 Illustration: Lasse Frank.

This illustration is an example of how we can accept deviations within certain limits, especially if we group them together based on the similarities they do share. The square shapes are different in size and proportion, but they all have four corners. The triangle with its three corners is therefore immediately perceived as standing out in the same context.

fits the figure', it says on the white page which, in addition to the text and an image of a biscuit package, only contains a summarily painted blue-toned bikini floating in empty nothingness. Where the 'figure' of the female body should be, there is nothing. However, the absent body is still present—we 'see' it anyway. Moreover, because of the accompanying text, it is very likely that we will 'see' a slim body, rather than a plumper one (Figure 3.6).

Focal point

Creating a focal point in a picture can be accomplished by using converging lines or vectors. Artists and designers of graphics and advertisements also use other methods to draw the eye to a specific focus. In an effort to capture people's attention they may, for example, use a colour that sticks out or place an unexpected object in a picture.

The Gestalt principles in contemporary use

Western society has a long tradition of seeking to create illusions within reality. We can find many examples of this throughout history, such as *Trompe-l`œil*,

FIGURE 3.6 Illustration: Lasse Frank.

The drawing is based on an advertisement for low-calorie biscuits from LU. The missing lines that represent the body allow the viewer to fill in the blank space on their own. Our ability to do this is thanks to our prior knowledge of what a body looks like. The point here is *what kind* of body is created by the viewer.

dioramas, stereoscopes and *Magic Eye* books which are printed so that the pictures can be perceived as 3D. Today, the technology of *virtual reality* (*VR*) can be used to create an immersive reality in art, games, and various other kinds of entertainment, as well as for purposes of education and training. Both VR and *augmented reality* (*AR*) technologies have attracted a lot of attention over the last decade. VR offers the possibility to create objects and environments that give the illusion of being real, making it possible to interact with objects, move about, and explore environments with a strong sense of presence. However, unless additional devices are used, VR does not offer any haptic feedback part from vibration. This presents a limitation when it comes to using VR for purposes such as interactive training and/or learning for assembly tasks since assembly is a physical performance that necessitates ergonomic considerations like weight, and involves complexity in the actual task (Eriksson et al., 2020). Studies indicate that users of VR experience a gap between VR and the real world. This contradicts the common idea that VR duplicates the physical environment and the objects in it, and that it is some kind of twin to a specific object or environment. Instead, we should regard VR as a re-presentation of an object and/or environment; it visualises aspects such as appearance, relationships and size, in much the same way as 2D visualisations. A VR environment exists with its own set of conditions, but it is also possible to discover a relationship to the physical world. In these contexts, the theories based on Gestalt principles are still utilised when creating VR environments and visualisations—whether or not this is done consciously.

It is interesting to keep in mind that Gestalt Theory, and the principles associated with it, were originally part of a more extensive interest in formulating theories related to what we consider to be visual communication today. Other initiatives included iconography, iconology, semiotics and semiology. This era of exploring, exploiting and explaining visual phenomena was, in turn, part of a greater interest in human physiology, including functions such as seeing, hearing and touching (Eriksson, 1998; Mirzoeff, 1995). Because of that, the expressions intended for audio, visual and physical touch mediums also became part of the science of the humanities. This interest was also expressed by visual artists. For example, one can see how interest in eyesight and vision in the late 19th and the early 20th century influenced and produced the visual art of that time. So-called pointillism, mentioned in the previous chapter, is just one example of a movement where artists experimented with painting coloured dots close to one another to melt them together and form shapes in the eye of the observer. In more recent times, artists such as Ellsworth Kelly elaborated with colours and shapes to thrill and puzzle the eye of the spectator.[2] We can find similarities to this in recent decades when considering the investigative approaches taken by the artists exploring digital technology for artistic purposes.

Meaning-bearing parts in visuals

Nothing in a picture lacks meaning. Regardless of the originator's intentions, the person who meets the picture, in whatever visual event, will read something into everything that is present in it—even if it is simply a brushstroke on a canvas. Here we can draw a comparison with written language. In grammar and morphology, a morpheme is a meaningful linguistic entity consisting of a word, like 'dog', or a word element, like the '-s' at the end of 'dogs', which cannot be divided into less meaningful parts. A morpheme is thus the smallest sentence unit in a language. In a similar manner, we must think of the lines, dots, colours, shades etcetera that appear in a picture—whether it is a photograph, drawing or painting—as meaning-bearing parts.

The reason we can interpret the same picture in a multitude of ways is that visuals have an open and simultaneous character. A visual is mainly ordered spatially on a surface, whereas written language is sequential and linear. Thus, we can decode a picture from any starting point. By contrast, when reading and decoding a text, we must start 'from the beginning'. In the case of a picture, for example, what one chooses as a starting point will likely be that which one finds to be most striking or interesting—whatever pops out in front of one's eyes. With that, the starting point works as a pointer that guides the reader in the interpretation of a picture. It could be something that was intentionally made by the artist or something that is of special personal interest. It could be either the most striking or the most familiar element. However, whether we are the producer or the interpreter, we also tend to follow cultural principles when coding and decoding pictures. In the Western tradition, we most often start reading a picture from the upper lefthand side before proceeding to the right, while in other traditions we read from top to bottom, or from right to left. Still, in visual communication, part of the 'usefulness' of a visual depends on the sender's ability to direct the spectator's attention and understanding. The sender may, for example, use the most awkward, the most familiar, the most sentimental, the most intriguing, or the most fearful signs and symbols in order to catch the eye—and hopefully the mind—of the spectator. Of course, what is perceived as 'the most', of any kind, is a question of cultural and discursive preference.

Characteristics of a visual

Previous sections discussed how the Gestalt principles influence the way we look at a visual and even what we look for. But what are the characteristics of a visual? We can view the world as a picture or as a text. If we consider the fact that pictures and texts constitute two different symbolic systems, what does it really mean to talk about pictures?

In contrast to verbal language, visuals are tangible. They can be either naturalistic or abstract in nature. Pictures can portray things as well as show relationships. What is unique about visuals is their mimetic function. (*Mimesis* is derived from the Greek verb *mimeisthai*, which means 'to imitate'.) Mimesis is thus used for the imitative representation of the real world in art. While words are created by letters or signs (e.g., the Chinese language), pictures are made up of parts that create a representation of specific or general individuals, environments or species. The particular characteristics a picture has makes it dominant in respect to how it impacts perception. Once we have seen something, it is hard to get rid of the visual impression. Even a mental image can be dominant. For example, when one reads a novel one can create a strong inner image of the milieu and the characters' appearances. So much so that, if one later sees a film adaptation of the novel, it can be very hard to accept the director's idea of what the characters look like. If one, instead, sees the film first and reads the novel afterwards, the appearance of the characters and milieu will most likely impose on the textual description. This is because one's own mental image does not fit someone else's mental image. Since it is difficult to ensure we share a common understanding with another person or group when discussing a matter, the use of visuals is useful. Our ideas and thoughts become exteriorised and tangible with help from a sketch or drawing, or a photograph of something we might be inspired by. Sometimes, even using a very simple sketch during a discussion or project planning session is enough to help a group of people align to the same understanding of a future state or result (Goldschmidt, 1992).

How can it be that we experience a picture as a representation of something specific? When we see an object or species, for example, we recognise its typical features. We can accept a stick figure as depicting a human, for instance, since the circle forms the head and the lines represent the other body parts. Just as important as recognising characteristic features is recognising the *form* of what we are perceiving. The form is something that exists in the physical surroundings, while the *shape* is a representation of the same thing but in two dimensions. When the object or a part of nature is represented on a two-dimensional surface, it is the subject's shape that makes it possible for us to perceive and recognise it.

For spectators, visuals can also create the illusion of presence. When looking *into* a picture, be it a photograph or a painting, one can experience that one is looking at one's grandmother or at the Tower of London, for example. Meanwhile, the fact that one is merely looking at a representation of one's grandmother or the Tower of London is ignored. During the artistic movement defined as realism, artists consciously created the sensation of being present in their paintings' compositions. This was achieved, for example, by only partly depicting a person within a group of people, recreating what one might see if one were sitting near the table in real life as an observer (Nochlin, 1971).

It might not be too farfetched to acknowledge the photograph's ability to accurately portray one's grandmother, since a photograph works with both the iconic and the indexical at the same time. But what does it mean to *look like* something? How come we perceive all the primary subjects in the pictures below as belonging to the same species? This is something that probably even a person without very much knowledge of horses would do, considering the horse's significant form and shape.

How is this visual sign communication different from or similar to written or spoken language? Even though we need to learn how to read a picture, it is still possible to recognise certain parts or items within it without understanding the complete meaning. The horse sculptures also allow for a multimodal experience, since they are low to the ground and accessible for children to sit upon. This additionally gives children the ability to utilise their previous experiences with horses (from reality, pictures or toys) which have informed them that horses are an animal they can ride. Even if one only has access to photographs of the sculpture, one can still recognise the subjects as horses. However, if one were to compare the sculpture of horses with a portrait of a specific horse, one would notice the difference. Even though the sculpture is the artist's version of horses, it is still possible to identify the subjects as horses. This is because the artist has created shapes and features that are relevant to all horses, such as the head, muffle, ears, tail and hooves. Thus, one can look at this sculpture and register each of the subjects as 'horse' without knowing anything else about horses or the artist's aim with the sculpture. However, if one has access to more specific knowledge about horses, one will probably recognise the difference between a pony and a big horse when looking at the sculpture and the portrayed horse (Figures 3.7–3.9).

FIGURE 3.7   Portrait of a horse.

Photography: John Samuel. CC Wikimedia.org.

FIGURE 3.8   A sculpture of two horses Daphne and Olle, by Aline Magnusson, 1992, Södermalm, Stockholm.

Photography: Anette Göthlund.

FIGURE 3.9   Pictogram of a horse Created by Hans Henningsson.

A picture can portray something specific, including its characteristic features, and, by that, show that which is generalisable. The pictogram showing a horse is *not* portraying a specific horse, while the sculpture is likely an interpretation of a specific pair of horses (by the names Daphne and Olle), and the photograph is a portrait of a specific horse. Photographs showing an environment, events, places and people are often interpreted as being specific, even if they are aimed at being general.

Photographs can also be used as metaphors. One example of this is a picture of a person climbing a mountain. Even though a specific person is portrayed in action, the purpose of this frequent motif in entrepreneurial settings, for example, is often to illustrate the act of challenging oneself and overcoming barriers. In the example here, we see the cover of an academic union journal. Bearing this context in mind, the climbing metaphor can be understood as meaning that one should accept support from others to help enable future career development (Figure 3.10).

FIGURE 3.10   Advertisement for the Swedish Association of University Teachers and Researchers, SULF.

"What does *your* future career look like?", asks the text.

Source: iStock, Getty Images.

As stated above, one of the complexities of interpreting pictures is that they do not offer any particular reading direction. We can, so to speak, 'enter' the picture from anywhere. By contrast, if we were to start reading a sentence from the middle we would probably have difficulties understanding the content. Some picture types, such as comics and instructions, depend more strongly than others on being interpreted in a particular order. If one were to look at a comic strip, for example, the reading direction one adopts—left to right or right to left, or from top to bottom—would depend on the culture one belongs to. However, within a single frame, there are often vague or zero indications of the correct reading direction. One knows which way to look from experience and, when looking at a comic strip, one is often guided by the next picture frame or the speech bubbles. However, the order in which the speech bubbles in the frames should be read might not be as apparent. If one were to miss something important in the previous frame, one would not understand the following one and would therefore need to go back and re-read the picture. Contrary to pictures, written texts decree a reading direction, and the structure of a text most commonly includes a beginning and an end.

Perhaps apart from certain kinds of poetry, spoken and written language depend on strict syntax in order to convey meaning. Therefore, we know where the text ends. The interpretation of pictures, on the other hand, is more complex since it is possible to focus on some details and exclude others. This also applies, in part, to how we read a text. A fairly general generalisation would be that there is a tendency for the reader to get better at guessing what is coming next in a word or sentence and that therefore reading speed increases slightly from beginning to end. It is also likely that the spectator will be missing details in the picture without noticing. This is due to the picture's ability to simultaneously present several different messages or stories. Accordingly, the spectator's full attention and interpretation skills are needed to fully comprehend the picture's meaning or purpose.

Regardless of what kinds of pictures we are dealing with, our attention is often directed by the details we recognise or which puzzle us; it could be something unknown or intricate (Ware, 2012). The detail that attracts our attention will also influence how we interpret the picture's message as a whole (Eriksson & Göthlund, 2004/2012). The nature of visual representations is ambiguous since the information or message is dependent on the reader's ability and motivation to interpret its meaning. Because of these complex characteristics, it is hard to talk about 'the content' of a picture; pictures are not merely containers filled with fixed content (Danto, 1999). Instead, a picture must be understood as a surface consisting of several elements that can be interpreted differently, depending on the person who is looking at it (Eriksson, 2017). There are several explanations for why the reader overlooks or leaves out parts of a picture. Since it is not possible to focus on the foreground and the background simultaneously, we oscillate between the foreground and background when looking at a picture (Rubin, 1915). In a picture that displays a lot of detail, we tend to keep our attention either on what is in the background or on what is in the foreground. However, sometimes it is not necessary to pay attention to every single element in a picture in order to grasp the overall information.

Imitating visuals

Since pictures display appearance and can show, for example, how to dress (e.g., in fashion pictures) or how to decorate one's home (e.g., in interior design magazines), they also offer instructions for imitation. The instructions differ depending on the intention of the pictures. Instructions—including information on how to cook, how to care for the environment or how to tend to one's body and health—can be understood as prompts for imitation. It is possible to imitate a picture without understanding the connotations of what is being depicted. Children, for instance, imitate adults by observing how they act and behave.

They imitate music artists and learn the most recent dance moves by looking at videos. Teenagers (as well as grown-ups!) learn how to apply make-up by watching tutorials on social media. Advertisements influence how we dress, what we eat, which cars we drive and so on. This kind of mimetic quality inherent in pictures, and the visual quality as such, is often something that we perceive and use intuitively, whereas a more systematic use of pictures is more complex (Eriksson, 2017).

To reach the intended target group for a piece of information, advertisement or work of art, it is necessary to take several aspects into consideration. Today, it tends to be more difficult to identify specific target groups since many societies are both heterogenous and complex Therefore, it is also a bigger challenge to foresee how different groups wish to identify themselves. There might be several identities present in terms of ethnic culture, religion, gender etcetera. This heterogeneity in our modern societies has made the task of figuring out how to gain the relevant authority with a set of instructions more demanding—whether the instructions are about how to use a specific medication or how to operate the latest vacuum cleaner model.

Advertisements have had, and continue to have, an embedded aim of instructing how we should behave. This advertisement by Nilfisk from 1960 speaks to a target group that was less diverse at the time. We see a housewife in a proper middle-class home with furniture that are up to date for that time. For some, this poster could be merely a kind of curiosities, something fun to put up on the wall. But if one decides to look at the picture more seriously and interpret it with a critical eye, one can find it to be full of preconceptions about gender, interior design and acceptable behaviour. That is, it is about class. The Nilfisk cleaner was aimed at women who were expected to look proper, even while tending to domestic duties (Figure 3.11).

They were to remain nicely dressed and only use an apron when cleaning or cooking. This image of the middle-class housewife shows the opposite of the working-class woman, who often used a duster or housecoat while cleaning the house (Figure 3.12).

Today's advertisements for vacuum cleaners might appear to be less interested in any specific user or target group. Instead, it is often the cleaner-as-a-product that is in focus, and one can find a variety of genders, ages and ethnicities that demonstrate its function—and, in this way, it reaches a wider consumer group. It can still be argued, though, that these less obviously normative visuals also communicate ideas and ideals of, for example, how one should live and with whom one should live with.

Interestingly, an initially domestic, Swedish company such as IKEA has become an international 'role model' when it comes to interior design, with its department stores arranged as showrooms for specific consumer groups. Likewise, on the internet, one can find inspiration for how to design one's home according to who one is or with whom one wishes to identify.

FIGURE 3.11 Advertisement for Nilfisk From Wikimedia commons.

The primary aim of this advertisement for Nilfisk is not to explain how to use a vacuum cleaner but, rather, to provide instructions on how one should maintain a middle-class home with a tidy housewife and well-cleaned surfaces.

FIGURE 3.12 Photography: Sten Didrik Bellander.

This picture from the same period as the Nilfisk advertisement is an advertisement for cleaning robes. It only shows the garment and cleaning tools while indicating when the robe is to be used, namely, when cleaning. The picture has also been part of the exhibition 'Folkhemmets mode' (The Fashion of the Swedish Welfare State) at Nordiska Museet, 2015.

A reason for the change in how companies address customers is that companies have grown increasingly aware of how visuals 'talk to us'. Today, if we do not feel we are being personally addressed, we are very rarely able to identify ourselves with a specific behaviour, product, or set of instructions. It makes us feel ignored and, therefore, we ignore the message. Role models are necessary for identification, and visual communication with the aim of reaching a specific target group relies on the members of that target group identifying themselves with a specific behaviour.

Schemata for interpretation

The need for models, or schemata, to be able to interpret visuals is an idea that is returned to throughout this book. It is connected to the laws of cognition (presented in Chapter 2) and, in this chapter, to theories on perception where we look for familiar forms that our eyes can use as a starting point in the interpretive process. Although the authors have emphasised that pictures do not offer a specific reading order, it has also been said that conventions exist which are implicit and that we learn how to use these reading conventions. This not only concerns the order in which we read something but also how we analyse and interpret different visual genres such as art advertisements and visual instructions. Some advertisements do not even show the specific products for sale, but merely display the brand name. Recognising what is actually being advertised requires that we are familiar with the genre as well as with certain consumption goods. The same goes for instructions for the assembly of customer products. Through all of this, we utilise whatever 'visual catalogues' we have access to which exist thanks to our previous experiences meeting and interpreting visuals in our everyday lives.

Previous experiences can help us to interpret visuals that are unknown to us. However, they can also cause us to *assume* what a picture is all about and, by that, mislead our interpretation. Some years ago, an assembly competition was set up by an assembly organisation as a fun activity for the participants. It was a complex assembly task, but the style of the assembly instructions was very simple, much like the instructions made for IKEA furniture. The participants were trained and skilled assemblers, and when they saw these instructions, their interpretation was that it was an easy task to solve. Therefore, most of the groups ignored the instructions, instead moving straight on to the task and, ultimately, failed to fit the parts together.

Visual representations of what is described as *digital transformation* provide an interesting example of how we search for previous visual knowledge and schemata. Digital transformation refers to the changes society undergoes as it becomes one where *Artificial Intelligence (AI)* and digital tools are expected to be integrated into daily life. Such visual representations are frequently created in the style of a *palimpsest*, consisting of visible layers where machines or human beings

FIGURE 3.13 Visualisation of the digital transformation.

This image is an example of visualising the digital transformation of society, where everything is imagined as being connected. Symbols of industry, online connectivity and artificial intelligence have been added to classic gear wheels.

are vaguely visible behind a blue dazzle.[3] We see an example of this in Figure 3.13. The gear wheels in the foreground represent the digitalisation, something one can deduce thanks to the text located in the centre gear wheel that reads 'digital transformation'. Interestingly enough, gear wheels are a mechanical construction, and their most common task is to transfer kinetic energy between rotating axes which means they have nothing to do with digitalisation. Instead, gear wheels are an old invention that dates back to 300 BC when they were used in Egypt. In this picture, each individual gear wheel represents a different part of the expected digital transformation such as AI, digital signals, and symbols for connections. Behind the blue dazzle, we see a man wearing a suit and tie and posing in front of a wall upon which it is possible to identify a map of the American continents and different diagrams. In one interpretation of this visual, the representation on the wall indicates a global market (with the maps symbolising 'global') and the gear wheels show how digitalisation contributes to linking parts together as well as how these parts impact each other. Using a feminist interpretation, the visual illustrates a traditional representation of a (business)man standing in the centre of development.

Visuals are used to support communication. But how do we find a common language to communicate about something that does not exist yet, such as future development? In this case, since we have no actual previous experience to rely on, visual metaphors are used to illustrate the digital transformation. Still, what often ends up happening, for example, is that the metaphors we use create a schema that, sooner or later, becomes 'common' in communication about 'the future'.

Decoding messages

Previously in this chapter, we discussed our ability, as well as our tendency, to look for patterns in an effort to orient ourselves and understand an environment and its artefacts. It is our way of making the things around us meaningful. A pattern is something that is organised and isolated. It can be formed on a piece of fabric or it can exist as part of a system. Furthermore, one could argue that a pattern on a piece of fabric is not an isolated phenomenon but, rather, belongs to a larger context having to do with the latest fashion trend or the design of the sofa and its context, for example.

We can recognise a pattern in a single visual artefact or among several artefacts, in a picture or in a television broadcast. But this does not mean that we fully understand the meaning of it. For instance, it is possible for one to recognise a map because of how the shapes and colours are organised into a pattern which one recognises as 'a map'. However, to be able to use a map, it is necessary to *decode* it. One needs to understand the *encoded* information in the form of symbols and an index. Encoding and decoding thus refer to the act of meaning-making. Having a message transferred into a conventionalised code is the encoding of the message. Or, as Stuart Hall puts it (1980), encoding is when a particular code becomes part of the semiotic structure of a visual. Decoding, then, is when the 'audience' actively engages in the process of 'making sense' of what is seen (or heard, experienced, etc.). In line with this thinking, it can be argued that visual culture is omnipresent in every civilisation; but this presence does not work as visual communication until someone acts upon it. Still, this does not mean that visual culture creates itself. It is created repeatedly by and among people in specific situations and environments, and is not necessarily always understood by everyone.

When we decode a visual, we are also able to embody its message and, by that, the visual becomes meaningful. We might internalise the message and reshape its meaning to become a part of our behaviour or identity. This will also become a part of our experience, something we bring with us and use when meeting other visuals and environments in the future. What is communicated through visuals can be *embedded* in the artefact or environment, while other visuals—such as warning signs, traffic signs or signs showing directions—express their purpose explicitly.

This example illustrates the concept. Looking at the picture (Figure 3.14) of the Pinner district of London's Borough of Harrow, it can be perceived as a neutral street environment. If one starts by describing the picture, one may identify older English architecture, including the entrance to a pub in the foreground and a church in the background. The street is empty of people but several cars are parked alongside it. Two signs are hanging from the arch that extends from the façade to the curb; one with the pub's name, Queen's Head, and another depicting a woman wearing a dress like those worn by women during the late 18th century. Three flags can be seen in the foreground: the flag of the United

FIGURE 3.14 A quiet street in Pinner, a suburb of London.

Photography: Yvonne Eriksson.

Kingdom, the flag of Europe and the rainbow LGBTQ pride flag. The three flags are visual signals explicitly expressed by the pub's owners, saying that they are for the EU and welcome LGBTQ people. To be involved in the visual communication act, one needs to not only notice the encoded visual information but also be able to decode these specific signs. By describing, analysing, and interpreting the picture, one puts things into words that would not otherwise be perceived by viewers. However, the photograph from the street communicates a frozen moment, something that can be decoded and analysed in retrospect, while walking along the street requires other forms of attention. In that case, decoding and interpreting the visual messages is a multimodal act which involves all the senses.

On the quiet London street, it is more likely that a visitor will notice the details in the architecture and the meanings of the flags than they would on a busy street in Bombay. In such an environment, the visual messages can feel overwhelming—especially if one is not familiar with the city.

Looking at a photograph and encountering the milieu *in situ* are, of course, two very different things. Those who are familiar with India and its tradition of delivering lunch boxes, can identify the men as *dabbawallas* and thus understand

FIGURE 3.15 Photography: Yvonne Eriksson.

The picture shows how dabbawallas organise lunch boxes before distributing them in Bombay, India.

that the photograph was taken in Bombay, where the system of delivering lunch boxes has been developed. (A dabbawalla is a person who works with collecting lunch boxes from people who have ordered lunch service) (Figure 3.15).

Those who are unfamiliar with the phenomena probably notice what is going on but without understanding, either looking at the picture or at the real-life scene if walking by that street. This is because the message is *embedded* in cultural codes which require a higher degree of familiarity with the phenomenon than more explicit messages.

When experiencing architecture, the perception of power is often present. One example could be the overwhelming cathedrals, which were built during the 13th century with the intention of showing the richness of God. But it could also be the huge entrances of 19th-century museums or schools, designed to communicate a sense of awe in front of the 'Cathedrals of Knowledge' of the time. These are examples of analyses of explicit communication in architecture. It is rarer to focus on mundane buildings, such as modern hospitals or healthcare centres. Consider, for example, how one might experience a waiting room in a healthcare centre that is well designed and furnished with comfortable seats versus one with odd, worn-out furniture and scraped paint on the walls. This is more embedded communication, indicating either respect or disrespect for the patients, the wealth or poverty of the centre—or both.

Key chapter takeaways

- The Gestalt principles that were formulated a hundred years ago are still fundamental today when it comes to understanding how we orientate ourselves visually in our surroundings—they explain why we tend to look for patterns, similarities and continuity.

- Every part of a visual bears meaning for the observer.
- In contrast to written language, a visual can be decoded from any starting point due to its open and simultaneous character.
- Pictures can portray and imitate appearances and settings, and people tend to imitate pictures.

Notes

1 Gibson, J.J. (1950). *The perception of the visual world*. Boston: Houghton Mifflin; Hochberg, J. (1962). Pictorial Recognition as an Unlearned Ability: A Study of One Child's Performance. *The American Journal of Psychology*, Vol. 75. No. 4, pp. 624–628; Mirzoeff, N. (2015). *How to See the World*. Pelican Introdution; Rose. G. (2016). *Visual Methodologies, An Introduction to Researching with Visual Materials*. University of Oxford; Ware, C. (2012). *Visual Thinking for Design*. Moran and Kaufman.
2 See https://www.moma.org/artists/3048
3 Palimpsest was originally a handwritten text on parchment where the text was erased so the parchment could be reused, even though the old text still slightly visible. Today it can be defined as something reused or altered but still bearing visible traces of its earlier form.

4

COMMUNICATION AND NARRATION

The relationship between communication and representation is a complex one. It is an ongoing cycle of meaning-making, interpretation and re-interpretation. As previously stated, language consists of signs and symbols which—according to common agreement—'stand for something' and, together, form a system of representation. Therefore, meaning, language and representation form a trinity. When talking about visual representation, however, the concept of representation actually means more than to 'stand for something'. The following chapter seeks to establish the idea that visual representation is also about agency. With every conversation, every story told—whether in words or in images—something happens that changes that which was before. New information is produced, feelings are set in motion, actions are initiated. There are several 'actors' in this: the sender or producer, the image or visual representation, and the receiver or spectator.

Communication as an interactive process

Communication is always an interactive process between a 'sender' and 'receiver', between pictures and individuals, between pictures, and between pictures and text. Communication *between* two or more subjects always requires a medium and a code. Although it is a basic concept in any communication theory, it is nonetheless important to highlight. We sometimes forget that a medium can consist of many different things. If one looks at a rock carving, for example, one can see how archaeologists have added red paint to what, originally, was only a shallow carving on the rock's surface, revealing the shape of a human foot, or the pit of a small bowl. This is done to make these symbols more visible. Thus, it is not only the stone that functions as a medium for communication but also the colour (Figure 4.1).

DOI: 10.4324/9781003170037-5

FIGURE 4.1   A photograph of a rock carving from Södermanland, Sweden.
Photography: Anette Göthlund.

Even though we can now clearly see the mark of a foot and small cavities, not even archaeologists are sure how to decode these messages from the late Scandinavian Bronze Age. In other words, we do not have access to the code key. There are, of course, a lot of speculations and ideas about all the different signs and symbols our forefathers have left behind in caves and on rocks. But still, nothing equivalent to the Rosetta Stone has been discovered to help us interpret these ancient messages today.[1]

The agency of the spectator

One of the arguments pursued throughout this book is the argument of activity and action. Looking at images is always an active process, performed more or less consciously.

According to early reception theories, the spectator is a passive receiver of a message, therefore, the audience studies of the 1950s were very much a discussion about the risks and dangers of mass communication, especially if the communication was visual, such as television and film. The impact of images and visual media was thought to be both stronger and more dangerous than text. This is because of the open character of the visual; meaning it is less of an unambiguous statement than a verbally formulated message. It was assumed that the audience was easy to manipulate since they had no way to protect themselves from the new media techniques. This phenomenon can still be seen today when, for example, new digital media is introduced and its potential dangers for users are discussed. This holds true for computer games, social media, VR and AI. Audience studies also became popular in relation to the 1980s cultural studies tradition and it was, above all, how different audiences reacted to watching TV that was of interest. However, Hall (1980, 1997) argued that any reading and de-coding of a message was the result of an active engagement with the message and the medium and performed on the basis of the individual's interests and intentions. Reception studies thus became more interested in the diverse ways different media communicated with, and was used by, different audiences. Instead of focusing on mass audiences, individuals' as well as subculture's understanding and meaning-making of the messages was of interest. Also, cultural studies expanded, and research influenced by feminist, gender and youth culture studies introduced further insights into the complexities of the message's 'receiver' (Radway, 1984/1991; Ang, 1985; McRobbie, 1991/2000).

Each communicative act is different from the next, depending on the sender, message, context, medium, technique, cultural background of the receiver/spectator, etcetera. This can be regarded as similar to Mirzoeff's concept of a visual event, introduced in Chapter 1. Here, the interaction between a spectator and an image is an ongoing process. Of course, the agency of the spectator in this process is connected both to the physical act of looking (one has the choice *not* to look, at least under normal circumstances) and to the interpretive act. How an individual interprets a certain visual message is related to all of the above-mentioned elements but, above all, it depends on the person's previous knowledge and visual experience; their visual literacy, as discussed in Chapter 1.

The agency of the producer and sender of a message is indisputable. Still, what is encoded might be decoded by the receiver much differently than originally intended. There are many ways for a producer of a visual message (e.g., an advertisement) to try to direct and control the possibilities of decoding; for instance, by using text as an 'anchor' (Barthes, 1964/1977) Still, a change of context and the extent of the spectator's visual literacy might produce a very different reading of the message than what was originally intended (Eriksson & Carlsson, 2022).

Agency of the visual

Images act. They do something with us and for us. They speak out in different tones of voice, languages and dialects. The concept of an *image act* was first introduced by Søren Kjørup (1974) as pictorial speech and his thinking was inspired by J. L. Austin's speech act theory, presented in *How to Do Things with Words* (1962). The use of language as speech not only conveys information, but is also performative: it leads to action. Through the concept of image act, we can understand how visuals exercise visual agency and how people interact with visuals by producing and consuming them.

However, according to the theories of art historian Horst Bredekamp, images are put not in the place of the words, but rather in the place of the speaker, so that the image becomes an acting subject. Bredekamp proposes that this view can be justified by the fact that images inherently possess effective power. It is the visual itself that generates an image act, rather than the spectator (Bredekamp, 2014, 2018). W.J.T. Mitchell argues similarly, stating that images are not simply passive beings or inert objects that convey meaning. Instead, images must be understood as animated beings with desires, needs, appetites, demands and drives of their own. They actually change the way we think, see and dream, as Mitchell reasons in *What Do Pictures Want?* (Mitchell, 2005).

Considering the role of visuals as similar to that of an act of speech can help us to understand how visuals also change the culture in different areas, such as the area of digital transformation. Since the digital transformation is partly ongoing, and partly a vision for the future, it is, in many ways, still unknown and therefore invisible. Still, media, companies, organisations, authorities and different kinds of steering documents distribute images of the digital transformation which suggest what a digitised society looks like. This imagery has an impact on the societal discourse—how society thinks about, perceives, and reacts to the digital transformation—and contributes to shaping our understanding of the future.

Creating imagery of the digital transformation is often accomplished by using visuals featuring huge cityscapes with blue light and white fluorescent squares forming grid-like structures; a representation of the enhanced connectedness that is expected to result from the digital transformation.

This feeds into the discussion on concepts: how can we portray something that we have no 'visual concepts' for? The image of 'the future', for instance, has long been reproducing what is, by now, rather fixed visual tropes. For example, the future repeatedly appears illuminated in blue light. At the same time, it might be interesting to imagine a future society that is not preoccupied with developing megacities. Not least because of the environmental movement and climate awareness, which seek to formulate alternative future societies. When we stand before the task of visualising the unknown, we have to reuse older visual conventions; for instance about 'the future', 'death', 'hell' or whatever we lack first-hand experience of. Thus, turning to history to model a contemporary image of the future (or death, hell, etc.) will, at the same time, say a lot about the historical period we take inspiration from and its imaginary worlds.

Visual communication in use

When discussing visual communication, it is necessary to consider all kinds of visuals and be aware of their various effects. Consider, for example, advertisements, photographs in different news media, scientific pictures, engineering drawings, pictorial instructions, picture books for children and fine art. These genres are not isolated. Instead, they influence one another—for example, concerning style and conventions—and also make conscious visual quotations of one another, especially in advertisements and fine art. This is what is referred to as *intertextuality* and *intermediality*.

When the richly illustrated French encyclopaedia by Denis Diderot and Jean le Rond d'Alembert was published in the mid-1700s, the engravings were made in a neoclassic style which dominated the fine art of that time. The illustrations in the folio volumes show the objects in context and use, but also in a disassembled state. The idea to use visuals to represent knowledge was not new at the time. The theologist and pedagogue J. A. Comenius illustrated his *Orbis Sensualium Pictus* already in 1682. This was an encyclopaedia intended for children, to help them get acquainted with the world through words *and* pictures. But representing objects in a disassembled state, organised in the picture plane, as in Diderot's and d'Alembert's encyclopaedia, was a novelty, and the greater audience met these kinds of representations for the first time. According to Denis Diderot, the aim of the *Encyclopédie* was 'to change the way people think' and for people to be able to inform themselves and know things. Diderot wanted to incorporate all of the world's knowledge into the *Encyclopédie* and hoped that the text could disseminate all this information to the public and future generations. This is part of the ideals of the Enlightenment: the democratisation of knowledge. It is interesting to consider the importance that was placed on the visuals' abilities to communicate this knowledge, since the general public was ignorant in reading visuals (Figure 4.2).[2]

Looking at the illustrations, it is interesting to imagine how the audience had to learn a new way of seeing. How did they make sense of six free-floating hands or the numbered illustrations of different objects? The aim to show something sequentially (first this, then that) but simultaneously, and to show both the tools

Bouchonnier.

FIGURE 4.2 An example from the *Encyclopédie* showing how to produce wine corks.

and the execution of the craft (in this case, how to produce wine corks) at the same time was a novelty. Moreover, the presentational structure itself—showing the items and grips both separately and in use within their context—is a way of communicating and conveying 'how to do something' which we have been embracing ever since. This visual tradition can also be observed in advertisements for fashion or furniture brands (in print and online), for example. One is shown a close-up view of a garment or piece of furniture in a disassembled state, and in a setting where it would be used.

When doing this—adding a setting, props, persons, etcetera—the message conveyed is no longer only about the specific product but becomes complex communication about ideals, norms, and more.

Modern-day engineering drawings used in manufacturing, as well as assembly instructions used by customers of IKEA and other ready-to-assemble furniture companies, for example, have continued to use this form of visual instruction, which consists of line drawings of disassembled objects and visual guidance on how to assemble the different parts. Some of these instructions (especially product instructions intended for customers) show enlarged parts to emphasise certain details, which makes the drawings even less naturalistic in a mimetic sense.

The instructions shown in Figure 4.3 are intended for furniture customers or, more precisely, buyers of a cupboard with drawers. They are divided into subsections that illustrate which parts should be assembled and how. To be able to execute the assembly, one needs to understand how to interpret the drawings, decode the information, understand what to do and then be able to actually do

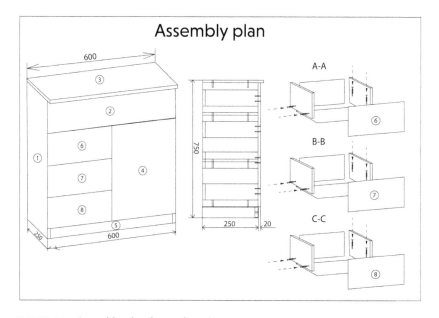

FIGURE 4.3 Assembly plan for cupboard.

it. By looking at assembly instructions from different decades—and centuries—it is striking how this pictorial tradition has survived over time. The fact that we can still face difficulties decoding and making sense of visual messages, whether we find them in an advertisement or a set of assembly instructions, shows just how much of this visual reading and decoding must be learned over and over again.

Drawings and models

When we talk about visual communication, we tend to overlook mundane visuals such as engineering drawings and models. These are expressed in a graphic language where grammar and syntax will only be understood by the initiated. The tradition of engineering drawings can be traced back to the renaissance architect Filippo Brunelleschi, who made drawings for the dome of the Cathedral of Santa Maria del Fiore in Florence in the 15th century (Ferguson, 1992). The engineering drawings aim to *show*. This is described by Ferguson:

> The drawings have two principal purposes. First, they show designers how their ideas look on paper. Second, if complete, they show workers all the information needed to produce the object. The information that the drawings convey is overwhelmingly visual: not verbal, except for notes that specify materials or other details; not numerical, except for dimensions or parts and assemblies. Such drawings, resulting from nonverbal thinking and possessing the ability to transfer visual information across space and time, are so constantly present in offices and shops that their crucial role as intermediators of engineering thought is easily overlooked.
>
> *(Ferguson, 1992, p. 5)*

Much of the tradition of visualisation that can be found in the context of engineering and the industrial sector is based on visual communication at a very specific level, with the purpose of showing both how different parts should be produced and how the products should be assembled. The way drawings and instructions are produced is based on traditions within the field but, most of all, it is based on the techniques that are available for producing and reproducing visuals. Figure 4.4 shows an example from the book *Five hundred and Seven Mechanical Movements* by Henry T. Brown from 1868. In these drawings, 507 of the small components that constitute complex machinery are presented and explained. Each component is meticulously portrayed so as to be as self-explanatory as possible to the reader. This book was widespread and still exists as a facsimile.

Today, many products are designed using 3D computer modelling. It is possible to elaborate on these models; one can zoom in to view small details, and zoom out to get an overview of the object, as well as rotate and shift perspectives.

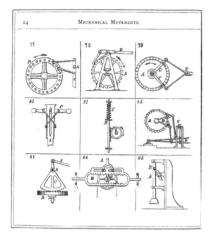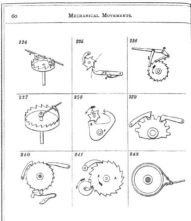

FIGURE 4.4 Example from *Five hundred and Seven Mechanical Movements*, by Henry T Brown, from 1868.

The aim is still the same as in Brunelleschi's time (to *show*) and, with that, the idea is to give the eye access to all that cannot be viewed simultaneously unless disassembled. Also, it still requires a certain kind of skill to be able to make sense of the picture, even if it appears as a photo with its mimetic qualities.

Drawings and models have also been frequently used in medical settings. The connection to norms and conventions in art history is more obvious here than in engineering visualisations. Engineers have been trained in the skill of drawing as part of their education from the beginning of the trade. This is because they need to be able to visualise and communicate their ideas. Medical students, on the other hand, learned to draw and sculpt and decode these two- and three-dimensional visuals as a way to study anatomy. In various atlases of the human anatomy from different times, it is obvious how art from a given period has influenced the appearance of pictures. When analysing anatomical visualisations, one finds that they follow the same conventions for how gender is expressed, for example, as the fashion images and art of the time. This not only depends on the prevailing view of science but also on the norms that exist for how the human body should and could be depicted medically, in combination with contemporary image influences.

Today, there is a large selection of human bodies available on the internet within the framework of medical research. One of the major projects from the early days of medical visuals on the internet was the *Visible Human Project*, in which dead bodies were scanned, millimetre by millimetre. Another example of a similar project is the Stanford Visible Female (SVF). The initial purpose of both projects was to create anatomical images that could be used in medicine, surgery and biomedical research. Nowadays, this technique is more developed, and it is easy to access these kinds of visuals. It might be easy to understand the representational norm of picturing bodies in parts as a functional choice. But there is also a long tradition behind it. Especially when it comes to depicting women's reproductive functions and genitals: they are often presented as loose parts, both in contemporary and historical illustrations.

In the illustration taken from William Hunter's publication, *The Anatomy of the Human Pregnant Uterus Exhibited in Figures* from 1774, we see how the woman has literally been portrayed as dissected. So much so, in fact, that the only feature that lets us identify a woman from these anatomical parts is the central image of a foetus in a womb. The foetus is presented as complete, and the carefully depicted body appears in sharp contrast to the mutilated and inflated torso framing it. The part of the female body depicted here brings to mind cuts of meat displayed on a butcher's counter. When *The Anatomy* was published, it revolutionised the study of the pregnant body. As the images in the book spread, physicians could see a realistic depiction of a foetus in utero for the first time. Due to its exclusivity, the work mainly circulated among the (male) medical community; the field of midwifery was largely female and not professionalised in the same way at the time (Figure 4.5).

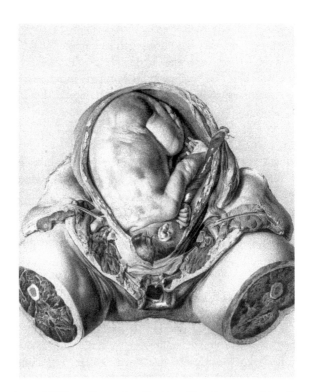

FIGURE 4.5 From William Hunter's collection *The Anatomy of the Human Pregnant Uterus*, 1774.

The significance of Hunter's image collection has been discussed in the essay titled 'Virtually Visible: Female Cyberbodies and the Medical Imagination'. Authors Julie Doyle and Kate O'Riordan (2002) address the historical analogy between SVF and Hunter's illustrations. The purpose of SVF's images is to show an accurate three-dimensional model of the anatomy of a female pelvis that can be used in operations. This has the consequence that the images medically only focus on parts of the female body, and thus the old tradition from Hunter's time is maintained where only fragments of the female body are shown.[3] If one compares the images from Hunter's time with today's high-tech projects, such as SVF, it is interesting to note that, despite the possibility to illustrate and show dynamic processes in images, the visual tradition of the Enlightenment has continued in which static fragments are displayed. When mapping out the human body, it has become the norm to look at each individual body part instead of focusing on the body as a whole. In this way, we continue to focus on the fragmented body.

Everyday visual communication

The environment that surrounds us is a hotbed for creativity that yields rich visuals, with people communicating using different kinds of pictures and moving images. Many of these visuals are so mundane in character that we hardly think of them as something we need to learn how to interpret or use. This includes gestures and body language, which also requires cultural awareness and knowledge. When engaged in mediated communication, such as trying to understand and follow visual instructions, it is impossible for one to correct misunderstandings that may occur in the same way as one does in face-to-face communication. Nevertheless, face-to-face communication is also complex and can be full of misunderstandings. But this can often be solved thanks to the ability to confirm whether one has understood correctly or not—not least by using multimodal communication such as facial expressions, the nodding of the head, gestures and so on. People meeting face-to-face to discuss things related to work and professional life often introduce some kind of modality or document as a platform for discussions, such as a drawing or text document.

These visuals can be produced ad hoc, in the form of a few hastily drawn lines on a piece of paper, for example. In meetings, whiteboards are often used to write keywords or describe or plan a process, with signs grouped and framed by circles or squares, and groupings linked by lines. If the aim is to visualise a process, this is likely accomplished with arrows drawn between groups of words. This kind of simple visual communication occurs frequently. However, the act is rarely defined as either a visual or communication.

Another example of this commonplace visual communication occurs when a guest checks into a hotel and asks the personnel at the front desk to recommend a nearby restaurant. The personnel often provide a free map and draw a circle on it to indicate the location of the restaurant, and then draw a line on the map to show how to get there from the hotel. Possibly, they ask the hotel guest to look for something specific, a landmark of sorts, like a building or monument, to be sure that they are on the right track. In this case, the hotel guest does not need to speak the local language but they do need to know how to navigate using a map. Landmarks such as monuments, buildings, rivers, and parks can thus be part of visual communication. They can be significant and recognised by many people, like Nelson's Column on Trafalgar Square, which has helped many tourists to find their way around London. But landmarks can also be very discrete, used only by a few (Lynch, 1960).

Signs calling for attention

There are types of visual communication connected to regulations or based on legislation that need to be expressed visually. Signs are used to designate something. They call attention to what to do or where to go. Or they indicate the contrary: what is forbidden. For example, signs indicating that one is not allowed to smoke in a specific area or bring along pets. These kinds of signs might show a picture of a crossed-out cigarette or a crossed-out dog. Or, in the case of the example pictured, it could be a sign containing the instruction to not let one's dog pee at the entrance of a building. Since the image only portrays a dog without a leash and is also placed at 'dog-level', one can wonder if the sign is directed at the dog itself! (Figure 4.6).

Signs can be slippery, which means that the same sign or symbol can be used for different purposes in different contexts. Therefore, it is essential to have access to the 'code key'. Take a map, for example. To be sure of the meaning of a dotted line, one must refer to the map legend. There, one can see whether the dotted line equals a trail or a small road. Even the simplest signs are open for interpretation due to the different cultural norms, literacy levels, etcetera of each spectator. Therefore, the cross used as an example above, and in many visual sign systems, is not as unambiguous as one might think. There is research showing how people's understandings of a cross differs. One example is a study where participants were asked to interpret a food product label featuring a pig marked with a cross to indicate there was no pork in the product. However, some of the participants interpreted this to mean that the food was forbidden for religious reasons, making the assumption that the product *did* contain pork (Strömqvist, unpubl.).

With other sign systems, there is no room for negotiation when it comes to interpretation. Take traffic sign systems, for instance. Traffic signs, as well as the lines on the road, support traffic rules which are regulated by law. Driving, biking and walking in a city are advanced acts of visual communication. Driving a car, for example, requires a highly skilled visual interpreter at the wheel. The driver must follow a multitude of messages from different signs while, at the same time, interpreting the traffic situation which includes trying to foresee the intentions of other road users. Adding to the complexity are different kinds of

FIGURE 4.6   The sign indicates that dogs are not allowed to pee on the entrance of a residential building.

Photography: Anette Göthlund.

roadside advertisements which often compete for the road users' attention. Still, since our sense of perception includes the ability to select what we are looking at, we can accept the visual noise and navigate the situation. The capacity to navigate within busy cities is something people have developed over time. It is a kind of connoisseurship to be able to select what to focus on in a traffic situation or to estimate the speed of an oncoming car or bicycle when crossing a street. It is interesting to imagine what the visual landscape was like only a hundred years ago, before high-speed traffic, advertisements and moving pictures were everywhere. It is also interesting to think about the capacity our human perception has developed in a relatively short period of time.

Tele-vision means far sight

Ever since television was first introduced and spread on the market in the 1950s, most people have been encountering moving images on a daily basis. This, of course, depends more or less on where and how one lives one's everyday life. Still, technological and digital development has profoundly changed the visual landscape.

The development of technologies, such as telescopes and X-rays, have made it possible for us to look far away into space or deep under human skin. Such technology is, in itself, a cornerstone for visual culture as we understand it. From the beginning, the use of this technology was reserved for scientists but, eventually, the public got access to it as well via various media such as television. The word television is derived from a mix of Latin and Greek roots and means far sight: The Greek 'tele' means far, and the Latin 'visio-n', means sight (derived from visio; 'vis-' means to see). It is difficult to envisage that it was not much more than one hundred years after illustrated magazines were first introduced to Europe, from the 1830s to the 1840s, that television became a common fixture in Western living rooms.[4]

Television created a visual genre in itself, even though it also incorporates movies, documentaries, animation and other visual formats. As spectators, we become familiar with news anchors and their ways of addressing us, as well as with their hairstyles and clothing. The news is often illustrated with either a background picture showing the place or event being reported about, or short, live-action videos shown in real time or recorded from the actual location or site of the incident. A news broadcast that lasts for about half an hour contains a multitude of visuals that communicate different aspects of various events. Examples include videos and photographs from war, which is a genre in itself that has its own traditions and conventions; moving images showing interviews with celebrities, politicians, and people on the street; and scenes showing the consequences of climate change: fires and floods, storms and hurricanes. Additionally, a lot of different, and often quite complex, infographics are used to explain or convey the weather statistics or election results.

Today, television as a medium and technology has, in many ways, lost its privilege both as a news medium and as entertainment. For many people, the computer screen has taken its place. Still, the visual conventions developed through the decades in television are also present on the computer screen. And, of course, the production style of newscasts, for example, does not necessarily change with the medium through which it is broadcasted. Together with other pictures we see in newspapers and on websites, these visuals are not mere representations of events and incidents. We experience the world through them, they work as a grid through which we come to understand reality. In this sense, they are co-creators of our subjective realities and we act upon them based on what we come to 'know' from them.

Visuals and emotions

Since visuals have agency, they also create emotions. They can put us in a specific emotional state, and we can use them to express ourselves or to affect someone else. A motif can work as a trigger for pleasure and lust or desire. Or it can be experienced as repelling and upsetting to spectators. These reactions can be spontaneous and direct, but the way we react to picture motifs is also based on conventions. We learn how to interpret and react to various kinds of visual motifs and how to comment and talk about their contents. The closest example at hand is, of course, various kinds of advertising campaigns. Working successfully with advertising is, to a large extent, dependent upon one's familiarity with how to engage with an audience on an emotional level.

In the history of fine art, we find many examples of visuals created with the intention of evoking or expressing emotions such as pleasure or fear to demonstrate power or to illustrate scary incidents or dramatic events. These communicative acts usually tell the history of an event and, at the same time, attempt to convey the feelings that event produced. The triumphant emperor returning from war on a muscular stallion shows his power both through his elevated position as well as through the manner in which he controls the animal. Throughout history, kings and popes have posed with uplifted chins and austere facial expressions, evoking a sense of exaltation. Today's world leaders may appear in other kinds of media, but the manner in which they express their power—for example, through body posture and personal appearance—is not very different. The fact that a majority of figures represented in visuals aimed at creating a sense of power or awe are of the male gender has not changed much either. Of course, power is also shown with economic wealth, perhaps symbolised by a palazzo featuring richly decorated ceilings and wall paintings or with a house drawn by a well-known architect. Whether the audience looks on in admiration or with fear depends on the relationship between the spectator and the subject portrayed.

Sculptures of heroes, such as kings and statesmen, affect people differently over time and their original function of symbolising power or honouring someone changes. At some point in time, the primary function of a sculpture may be as a landmark, merely a place to meet up with friends. Then it might come to life again, for instance, when the political environment changes. The posthumous reputation of kings and commanders changes according to shifts in politics and current events. Throughout history, we find several examples of iconoclasm where monuments have been destroyed in response to changes in the religious or political system. It happened in Ancient Egypt when the recently instated pharaoh Akhenaton introduced a new religion to the empire, and it happened in the former Soviet states in 1989 after the fall of the Berlin Wall. Trying to forget or hide a hurtful historical past has resulted in torn-down buildings as well as sculpture cemeteries. In Budapest, Memento Park hosts a variety of sculptures and monuments that have been deemed obsolete either by public opinion or political powers (Figure 4.7).

More recent examples can be found in the debates following post-colonialism and other repressive politics and ideologies, such as the protest movement Rhodes Must Fall, which began in Cape Town, South Africa in 2015. This protest movement originated around a statue commemorating Cecil Rhodes which was located on the University of Cape Town campus. The British mining

FIGURE 4.7 From the Memento Park in Budapest, with a statue of Lenin in the foreground.

magnate Rhodes was the prime minister of the Cape colonies between 1890 and 1896 and, to many South African citizens, he represented imperialism and colonial power. The call for taking down the statue was seen as a metaphorical call for the transformation of the university's curriculum, culture and faculty, which many black students felt were alienating and reflected a Eurocentric heritage.[5]

Language as narration and memory

Narratives play many different functions in human lives. In the theoretical literature, narration is often described with terms such as *events, functions, sequences, temporality* or *causality*. Monika Fludernik (1996) instead uses the term *experientiality*. Experientiality refers to the ways in which a narrative taps into a reader's familiarity with experience (according to Fludernik's thinking) through the activation of cognitive parameters, such as perception of temporality and the emotional evaluation of experience (2003). Building on Fludernik's theory, we can understand *visual* narration as a cognitively grounded relationship between human experience and human representation of experience, where visuals of all kinds are used. Hence, narratives are an integral part of the human experience, and storytelling is part of who we are and how we make meaning of the world. Experiences are collected and converted into memories. These memories are also used for the telling and re-telling of who we are.

The act of reflecting and telling can also be understood as how we make the unfamiliar familiar. It can be an experience we cannot grasp, an image we cannot make sense of or a visual we do not understand. If we do not immediately recognise what we see, we start to search deeper in our memory, tentatively attaching words to the visual phenomenon. There might not even be an utterance—the 'silent language' in our heads also helps us to see and understand what we see.

How we talk about visual representations is influenced by our native language and what words and concepts are available in that specific language. An important part of verbal language is its ability to create *concepts*. Concepts differ from words since they are formed by mental images or ideas; they can be something abstract. We use words when describing a mental image or a picture, but we need to be specific in our communication. For example, in a medical context, there are certain concepts developed within that discourse or, as in the previous example of engineering drawings, where technical competence is required. If one does not have access to the concepts, it is very hard for one to communicate what one is referring to in an efficient manner. When new phenomena appear, or if we find ourselves in front of something we do not recognise or have no previous experience of, how can we identify what we see in front of us? We try to match this 'unknown' to the schemata that are available, but if this fails, we face a communicative challenge. The spectator who meets new visuals, objects or phenomena looks for similarities, trying to match the unknown to already known categories.

In accordance with the semantic meaning of words, the grammar of a narrative must be coherent so that the audience can fully understand the story's significance. Pictures support a story, but they also require some explanation so the audience can use them to understand the overall message. Thus a narration can also support a picture.

Before we can interpret what we see and perceive, we must always begin by grasping the content of a picture—that is, what is *actually visible* in the picture. We can compare this to how one performs a basic picture analysis, starting with identifying the different elements of a picture on a denotative level. Only then is it possible to attempt interpretation on a connotative level in terms of what we see and what sense we can make of it. This means that the content is also created by the description. In a description, we utilise memory and previous knowledge and experience. This relationship becomes clearer when looking closely at the example of a typical still life painting from the mid-17th century by the Dutch artist Willem van Aelst (Figure 4.8).

A group of fruits are arranged against a dark, almost black background, and are partly embedded in leaves and twigs. If one looks closely, it seems the arrangement is resting on a horizontal surface draped in a black piece of fabric. The way the artist has worked with white paint to create highlights against the dark colour creates the illusion of a smooth, shiny textile. When one's mind begins to try and identify and define *what kind* of textile might be portrayed, experience and knowledge of textile materials, however mundane, are needed. It is likely many know that a piece of linen cannot create the same reflection as velvet or silk, for

FIGURE 4.8 *Still life with peaches and grapes* by Willem van Aelsted, Nationalmuseum. Photography: Erik Cornelius.

instance. Therefore, it is possible to conclude that it is either silk or velvet depicted in the painting. Identifying the fruits is equally dependent on what one knows about fruit. The round shape and the different shades of red and yellow might give the idea that these are apples. But the painstakingly thorough depiction of the different textures of the fruits can also assist one in using one's sensory memory of what it feels like to hold an apple as compared to the soft, but slightly hairy peach. One may recognise the cluster of smaller fruit as grapes. Mostly due to their size. Blackcurrants, for instance, are smaller. There is an almost dusty quality to the white coating partly covering each grape. It is almost possible to feel the stickiness a grape would leave on one's fingers if one were to pick it. One of the grapes has a different shape. One probably knows what it tastes like to bite into one of those. It has started to rot. Looking at these fruits, which may trigger one's memories related to smell, taste and touch, can help one to identify their correct names. It is also possible to notice something that probably no one is keen to eat: a small snail and a fly. These insects are, of course, unwelcome in a fruit bowl. But what are they doing in the picture? To decipher their meaning, a different kind of knowledge beyond the everyday understanding of fruits or insects is needed. For someone who has studied art history and iconography (the study of traditional or conventional images or symbols often associated with a religious or legendary subject) the addition of the snail and the fly, as well as the rotten grape, might turn the picture of delicious fruits into an image of *vanitas*, a visual trope often used in still life paintings as a reminder of the transient nature of life. If the snail and the fly were to be omitted from the description of this picture, it would be a completely different story. It could even be seen as an old-time advertisement for fruit.

This is all to say that there is an indissoluble relationship between content and description, between form and meaning, which goes in line with Mirzoeff's (2015) statement that visual culture is the relationship between what is visible and how we verbalise what we see (p. 11).

Speaking of memories

There is a difference between assigning a name to an object or visible phenomenon and describing something visible by building up entire sentences through which the narrative is constructed. When we look at a picture, we normally start to think about it and, in doing so, formulate what we are looking at. We notice some details and miss others. As shown above, memory is involved when we look at a picture or visual scenery. Memory can be divided into three categories: *working memory*, *semantic memory* and *event memory* (Baddeley, 2003). We involve our working memory when we look at pictures and/or read text; it is because of the working memory that we can process multimodal information. Semantic memory has to do with knowledge, and event memory is connected to something we have experienced. When we look at pictures, often all of these aspects of memory are involved; and it is from that starting point that we begin to talk about the picture in front of us. We look at a picture and consider whether it is something that we recognise or have knowledge about and if so, we may relate it to some experiences or specific situations.

When taking photographs in a specific situation, we can only focus on one or a few things that we see in front of us at a time. Meanwhile, the camera registers much more than we do. For example, looking at the photo in Figure 4.9 at the moment it was taken, focus was placed on the motorbikes. The picture was taken in Taipei and now that it has been taken, one can look at what was happening in the actual moment, but one cannot return to that moment. The moment is dead, according to Barthes (1981) but one can still create a narrative based on the memory of the event when one was standing at that intersection.

When we start to talk about a picture, re-tell the moment it captured or think about it, we are simultaneously creating a story. This narrative about the picture creates a grid between the us as the viewer and the actual picture in the same manner that any representation—textual, spoken words or visual—inserts a distance and an interpretation between the audience and the 'actual event'. This is why we can never state that a picture—nor even a photograph—mirrors reality.

FIGURE 4.9 Street view from Taipei.

Photography: Yvonne Eriksson.

There are too many layers of personal, but also cultural, utterances that exist in between the image and the spectator.

When we recall a situation or event, memory plays a crucial role. And when we formulate a memory, we use words. Memories are often influenced by visuals or visual scenes, but these cannot be communicated directly and are therefore described verbally. Apart from the fact that not even photographs can be said to 'tell the truth', they can, in a certain sense, give us proof—in this case, proof that the event in Taipei actually occurred: 'I was there'. Consequently, we can regard photographs as souvenirs of specific moments. In this case, the scenery from the street in Taipei. If we instead, consider a painting or drawing of the same event and street scenery as similar to a modern version of the *veduta*, this would add yet another level of interpretation.[6] This is because the artist's choice of perspective, light, colours, brush strokes, etcetera would add several layers of visual meaning between the actual event and the visual representation or re-telling of it. Most probably, this would affect the original memory one had of standing at the inter-section of a busy street in Taipei, waiting to cross. Even if the artist happened to be the same as the person crossing the street.

Another kind of storytelling

We have already touched upon the performative aspects of visual communica-tion as well as the fact that communication, in any mode, is a transformative pro-cess. A performative act where something happens, changes or is set in motion. Every visual event, visual encounter and use of visual expressions has a performa-tive aspect. Especially if we stick to the idea of the image act and that visuals have agency, *performativity* becomes a given ingredient in the discussion on how visual communication works. The meaning of perform is 'to act'. And it is in the moment of the performance that 'it comes into existence'—'it' being the meaning of a visual message, or the 'me' as presented to others (Goffman, 1959; Butler, 1990).

A traditional photo album or, more recently, an Instagram feed, may be shown to new acquaintances as a way of introducing the family history or creating a story about a person. But it might also be shown over and over again within a family as a way of reactivating the memories and feelings of 'who we are' and strengthening a sense of togetherness. Thus, storytelling is also about how we want to present ourselves and our lives to other people. Often, we co-create the stories in a manner of conversational storytelling. Something that also occurs when using visuals. Social media may have become the most important arena for presenting ourselves visually. There are many different ways to create numerous stories of the life one has—or one's life as it should be. Several platforms offer possibilities to create events and stories or share a video. The possibilities to represent our experiences and present ourselves are endless.

Many different types of narration exist. One type of narration, which is rarely regarded as either visual communication or storytelling, is financial presentation. For instance, a financial presentation might be used for an annual company report. Since co-referencing creates visual continuity, the method can be deliberately used to exploit an audience's ability to create a coherent story from a presentation. This is achieved by including clear references between the presentation slides; for example, in the form of a uniform scale chart. It is vital that various elements in each individual slide or picture have a clear relationship to the previous slides. However, if the presenter is unaware of co-references and how the concept works, they can unknowingly create a story that leads to misunderstandings. Or a presenter could knowingly use co-references to manipulate their audience. Presentations that show charts with their various contents in a sequential manner can create a story that is either coherent or contradictory, depending on how well the presenter depicts each chart's relationship to the whole. A common claim is that statistics lie. But it is much more plausible that the manner in which the statistics are presented, either in an individual chart or a range of charts, is what makes misinterpretation possible in the first place (Figure 4.10).

The infographic is a widely accepted form of visual communication and is considered to be something neutral that only consists of facts. A chart is an effective way to display large amounts of data and demonstrate relationships. It is excellent for providing a quick overview. Research indicates that people tend to experience and understand the same data differently depending on what type of format it is presented in, be it a line or bar diagram (Zack & Tversky, 1999).

Today, it is easy to enter data into an Excel sheet and automatically create various kinds of charts. Data from a study with a limited number of participants can be used to generate graphs, bar charts and pie charts that show percentages and convey a relevant picture of what was researched. This is widely known

Viltolyckor med vildsvin i Södermanland – 2021

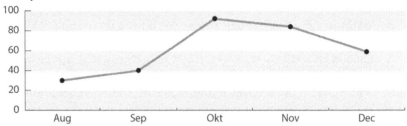

Viltolyckor med vildsvin i Södermanland – 2021

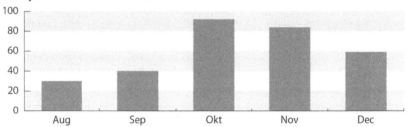

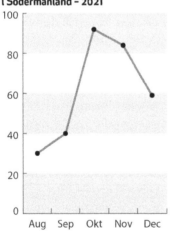

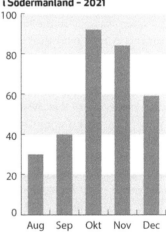

FIGURE 4.10 Illustration: Lasse Frank.

Four diagrams showing the same number of wild boar accidents from August to December 2021. The design of the diagrams lead us to believe that the different versions contain different information.

but, still, it can be tempting to use Excel charts to produce irrelevant results. A researcher must also decide whether they will design a chart that is demanding for the reader in terms of comprehension, but provides a deeper understanding of the findings, or if they will design a more easily comprehensible chart featuring a more basic representation of their findings. However, an infographic is a very complex form of visual communication; not even in these seemingly simple examples is there any such thing as neutrality in connection to how they are represented. Each infographic is the result of many subjective considerations and choices made by the producer.

Visual storytelling and the function of focalisers

In still pictures, visual storytelling can be found in a visual showing several scenes (in simultaneous succession), or one single scene. Or it can be found in a comic strip where several frames create a storyline. An example of the former is the Bayeux Tapestry.[7] This was probably commissioned in the 1070s by Bishop Odo of Bayeux, the half-brother of William the Conqueror, and shows embroidered figures and inscriptions comprising a representation of the conquest of England. It is over 70 metres long and, although it is called a tapestry, it is in fact an embroidery. The border of the tapestry depicts lions, birds, camels, minotaurs, dragons, sphinxes, some fables of Aesop and Phaedrus, drawings of agriculture and hunting and so on. To be able to grasp the whole story depicted in the tapestry and to perceive the content on the tapestry's border, one must walk alongside it. This tapestry, featuring several parallel narratives told in many scenes, is only one example of a pictorial tradition that can be found in visual cultures in different parts of the world.

In line with the semantic meaning of words, the grammar of a narrative must be coherent enough that the audience can fully grasp the significance of the story. Images can support a story, but they also require a certain degree of explanation so that the audience can use them to understand the overall message. For example, Bal (1985) explained how a *focaliser* can lead a viewer through a story (Bal, 1985). A focaliser exists on two levels: as the illustrator or graphic designer who frames the story and chooses which (or whose) perspective to tell it from; and as the narrator in the image who uses gestures and body language to indicate what the audience should focus on. Of course, it is the creator or artist who decides how to install and use the focaliser(s). But in the image itself, we can see how the use of body posture, angles, light, etcetera direct the spectator's eyes and attention.

In Caravaggio's *The Calling of Saint Matthew* (painted between 1599 and 1600 for the church San Luigi dei Francesi in Rome), a story is told in one picture frame only. The painting depicts the story from the Gospel of Matthew (Matthew 9:9): 'As Jesus went on from there, he saw a man named Matthew sitting at the tax collector's booth. "Follow me," he told him, and Matthew got up and followed him.' Caravaggio depicts Matthew the tax collector sitting at a table with four other men. Jesus Christ and Saint Peter have entered the room, and Jesus is pointing at Matthew. It is almost overly explicit how the light streaming in through the window in the upper right corner works together with the uplifted hand—which is said to be the hand of Peter directing our eyes to the pointing finger of the old man—to reach the figure of a young man sitting at the end of the table with a lowered head, dealing with the coins on the table: Matthew. The

FIGURE 4.11 *The Calling of St. Matthew*, by Caravaggio, 1599–1600.

light thus serves a double function. It is a focaliser in that it is pointing towards Matthew, but it is also a focaliser within the story itself (Figure 4.11).

If one begins to analyse visuals—ranging from historical paintings to modern-day advertisements—one will find that the use of focalisers is common. Going back to the discussion in Chapter 3 and the examples from Gestalt theory, it is obvious that when artists learn how to guide our perception, using vectors for example, it proves to be an efficient technique for controlling the narrative.

Key chapter takeaways

- In visual communication, agency must be attributed to both the spectator and the visual itself. This forms the basis for visual communication, since communication is an interaction between spectator and visuals, between visuals and visuals, and between spectators and spectators.
- The way we talk about pictures is related to our mental images and memories.
- Narratives, including visual narratives, are an integral part of the human experience, and storytelling is part of how we make meaning of the world and who we are.

Notes

1 The Rosetta Stone, found in 1799, has a message carved into it, written in three types of writing. When it was discovered, nobody knew how to read ancient Egyptian hieroglyphs. Because the inscriptions say the same thing in three different scripts, and scholars could still read Ancient Greek, the Rosetta Stone became a valuable key to deciphering the hieroglyphs (https://blog.britishmuseum.org/).

2 *Encyclopedia, or a Systematic Dictionary of the Sciences, Arts, and Crafts*, was a general encyclopedia published in France between 1751 and 1772. Engraver Robert Bénard provided at least 1,800 plates for the work.

3 *The Anatomy* was illustrated with engravings by Jan van Rymsdyk (c. 1730–c. 1790) and other unknown artists.

4 In 1842, British news agent Herbert Ingram created one of the first illustrated magazine: *The Illustrated London News*. For the illustrations the technique wood engravings were used.

5 As stated by Adekeye Adebajo, Executive Director of South Africa's Center for Conflict Resolution, in BBC News Magazine 1 April 2015.

6 A *veduta* (Italian: 'view') is a detailed, largely, but not necessarily, factual painting (drawing, or etching) depicting a city, town, or other place. The first *vedute* were probably painted by northern European artists who worked in Italy, such as Paul Brill (1554–1626), a landscape painter from Flanders who produced marine views and scenes of Rome that were purchased by visitors. Much like the postcards from the 1900s. Another very famous *vedutisti* is the venetian Canaletto (Antonio Canal, 1697–1768).

7 https://www.bayeuxmuseum.com/la-tapisserie-de-bayeux

5

CONTEXTS, SITUATIONS AND FRAMING

A *context* can be defined as the circumstances that form the setting for an event, statement or idea. Such circumstances are not static, but rather arise through an interaction that takes place between, for example, a spectator and visual objects. Therefore, a context should be understood as a *situated action* (Costello, 2014). Interactions, situations, as well as socio-cultural aspects are dynamic and change over time. Therefore, the manner in which spectators are affected by what they encounter is hard to predict. In the same line of thought, the feminist art historian Griselda Pollock describes context as plural in the sense that it is not possible to talk of only one context; several contexts are present at the same time (Pollock, 1999). If we consider a picture, for example, a context for the creator of the picture, a context for the production of the picture, a context for the appearance of the picture, and a context for the viewer of it all exist simultaneously. Some of these contexts are not always obvious. They can be hidden behind assumptions about the conditions for the production of the picture, or assumptions about the creator or spectator. In this chapter, we take a closer look at the differences between contexts and situations, and why it matters to make that distinction. The multifaceted concept of 'framing' is also discussed, since framing is an important factor when it comes to making sense of visual and other events in our everyday lives.

Contexts and situations

To understand how a context is created by situated action, we can consider how the context in which a picture comes into being not only places the artist, photographer or illustrator in a socio-cultural context, but also places them in a historical or contemporary context. The creator themself also belongs to

DOI: 10.4324/9781003170037-6

several contexts; for example: their socio-cultural background, their contemporary position as an artist, and the artistic tradition they belong to. The visual artefact is created under specific circumstances, in a studio for example, and is then displayed before a broader audience in a gallery, magazine, book or online. It travels from a domestic sphere (the studio of the creator) to a public context. When Griselda Pollock (1999) introduced and discussed context as being plural, she did so for a specific purpose; namely, to contextualise not only the work of art but also the artists and their cultural traditions and cultural belonging. From that starting point, it becomes possible to map out the canon. That is, the general criteria for what has been accepted as great art and, by that, to elucidate the power relationships within the history of art.

The discussion about context goes in line with what Gillian Rose (2016) presents as a model for the *sites* and *modalities* used to interpret visual materials. In Rose's words, the sites include the site of production, the site of images itself, the site of circulation and the site of the audience, or *audiencing*. The modalities include the technological modality (how a visual material is made), compositional modality (the specific material quality of a visual object) and social modality (the social, economic, and political relationships that surround a visual object). Consequently, the context of a visual is multilevel and influences how we perceive and interpret both the visuals themselves and the environment in which they appear. There is also a distinction between inner and outer context. The inner context of a visual concerns everything that appears within the picture frame: how the different picture elements are arranged in the picture and how they relate to each other. The outer context, contrastingly, consists of the surrounding environment: the room, cityscape, book or magazine where the visual appears. Just like the title of an art piece, any associated text is also part of the outer context.

If we consider visual communication as an act of looking and displaying, then visual communication is inherent in nature. Plants, animals and birds also use visual communication with us (if we notice it), as well as with each other and other species. The bright colours of a flower signal its welcome to the bee so it can be pollinated. The seasons are visible in nature, the trees shift colours, and the species of flowers in bloom vary depending on whether it is spring, summer or autumn. The birds come and go over the year. What and how nature communicates is something we as humans need to learn in order to regard it as an act of communication. From the perspective of nature itself, it is not communication but rather embedded information.

Visual artefacts such as illustrations, models and paintings showing parts and details from nature are, of course, to be considered visual communication. If we look at a handbook on birds, for example, we will likely find it consists of both illustrations and texts describing different bird species. First of all, we have the bird itself that lives in a specific place and under certain conditions. This must be recognised by a photographer or an illustrator. A photograph of a bird is a representation of a specific bird that is unique and the bird is depicted in a defined environment. On the other hand, an illustration, such as a drawing or painting, creates a generic image for all the birds of this species, showing what is characteristic of a bird of this kind, including its environment. Unless, of course, it was made with the intention of portraying that particular bird-individual. The aim of an illustration in a handbook of birds is to provide support in identifying and looking for particular bird species in nature and, therefore, the illustrations emphasise the characteristics of each bird. Yet another example can be found in a children's book that aims to facilitate learning about the most common birds in Sweden. The illustrations in such a book must represent all the specific charac-teristics of each species while, at the same time, appearing playful and not overly complex (Figures 5.1–5.3).

FIGURE 5.1 Robin.

This photograph of an individual robin was taken at a specific moment.

Photography: Kim Forchhammer.

FIGURE 5.2 Robin.

Birds are depicted in different ways depending on the purpose and context. The following exam-ple shows a picture of a robin taken from a bird handbook. The picture shows the characteristic features of a robin.

Illustration: Karl Aage Tinggaard.

FIGURE 5.3 Robin.

This picture is from a children's bird book and, although the robin has the appearance of a sto-rybook picture which one can expect to find in a children's non-fiction book, it shows the key characteristics of the robin.

Illustration: Jonas Källberg.

So, we have the context for the bird (nature itself), and the context for its representation (the book or the photograph). The audience of the pictures will likely be diverse. Some will look at the pictures for pleasure; others to learn about the birds with the motivation to study birds in nature. This is the context of the audience or the site of audiencing. The inner context of the illustrations could be the handbook, while the outer context, in that case, could be in the reader's home or outdoors in nature itself.

If we continue to consider the context as something that exists in the plural, we also need to explore the context in relation to one or more situations. In a specific situation, the context may be less important since the situation will put the context in the background. At first glance, handbooks featuring photographs of birds, flowers or mushrooms give the impression of being easy to use for identifying the species in nature. However, the photographs—with their capability to accurately represent moments—will sometimes hinder the perceivers' ability to notice the species in other settings or situations. The situation in which the handbook is used will overrule the context since the focus is on comparing the visual representation of the bird, flower, or mushroom with its real-life counterpart.

Situations

A situation can consist of either a brief moment or a longer time span. Even though a situation can dominate over the awareness of context, it is nevertheless an inherent part of the context. Several individuals can share the same context while, at the same time, being in different situations. In the context of a historical art museum, for example, the art teacher visiting with a group of art class pupils is in a different situation from the pupils, as well as from the elderly couple strolling peacefully through the halls. The museum staff find themselves in yet another situation, with the duty to, perhaps, handle restless kids or help the elderly couple locate the Rembrandt. The context of the art museum offers a certain way of experiencing art. Its architecture, the way in which its interior is designed, the manner in which the artworks are displayed, how the staff perform their duties—all of this is part of a well-established museum discourse and forms the context for a museum visit. Still, no two museum experiences or visual encounters will be identical, since the situation of the individual visitors vary. This influences not only how the visitors interpret the meaning of the visual representations in the museum, but also which representations they will recognise. It is possible that the kids are more aware of the museum's sign pointing towards the cafeteria than the signs directing them to early Netherlandish paintings.

A painting of a historical event is often made for a specific reason. It could be to glorify a person or commemorate a historical incident, or perhaps to critique one or the other. If the painting is created by a renowned artist, it will probably be displayed in a central part of the museum and included in the catalogue of the museum collection. In that context, the painting will be regarded as a historical art artefact and analysed from this vantage point. This means the skill of the artist, the composition of the painting and its style will be appreciated, and its iconography interpreted. If the painting appears in a history textbook, it will most likely be used as an illustration of a historical event and it might even function as a historical source. In this context, the reader will probably not take the art's historical aspects into consideration. Looking at the inner context, the textbook influences the interpretation of the picture, but so does the situation. If the reader, say a pupil, is focusing on reading in a relaxed moment, it is more likely that they will look at, and perhaps even enjoy, the picture. But if the pupil is feeling stressed, the appearance of the picture could merely be experienced as a relief since it minimises the number of pages that must be read by the next day.

Where the visual encounter occurs

As with Rose's site of audiencing, the context in which a visual appears also influences how we perceive it. If we are looking for something specific in a public space, for example, we pay attention to signs of a specific kind that can guide us towards what we are looking for. When looking for a toilet in a public space, it is a situation in which one rarely analyses the sign indicating there is a toilet. Most of us have learned to understand which sign indicates the women's and the men's toilet, respectively. The three signs shown in Figure 5.4 have different meanings, even though they all indicate that a toilet exists behind the door. Signs for 'toilet' or 'restroom' are built around conventions. Interestingly enough, there is no symbol of an actual toilet in these pictures. This means that the signs

FIGURE 5.4 Pictograms indicating toilettes for men, women, and gender-neutral usage.

shown here could also indicate a dressing room, for instance. In this case, it is the location, situation and context together that help one find the right facility. The sign for the women's toilet is a pictogram showing a figure wearing a dress, and the one representing the men's toilet is a figure wearing trousers. The one to the left indicates a women's facility, and the one in the middle shows that it is a facility for both women and men, while the one to the right has the ambition of indicating the toilet is gender-neutral by displaying a third figure partly wearing a dress, and partly trousers. Conventions for how to represent gender are strong. Therefore, we are stuck with the trousers and the dress as symbols for 'man' and 'woman'. The way pictograms are designed often make one blind to such conventions. On the other hand, it is the stereotypical appearance that makes it easy for one to recognise the aim of the pictograms. The 'gender-neutral' pictogram shows that it is nearly impossible to show the concept of gender-neutral in pictures because the conventions are so strong—we do not have a visual language for that.

Furthermore, one can also assume that the spectator's profession and cultural background impact how they perceive and interpret the visuals above. If, for example, one has not been exposed to discussions on whether such phenomena as 'gender-neutral' or 'cross-gender' exist, the sign featuring the dress-trouser-attired man/woman might be confusing. So, to understand how seemingly unambiguous visuals can be understood, we need to consider contexts with regard to the recipient, the environment and where the visuals appear; and with a focus on both the outer and inner contexts, and the context in which the actual visuals were created.

Unless we reflect upon how gender and culture are created and communicated in various kinds of visual representations— e.g., in fashion photography—or upon how professions are depicted, it is easy to accept them as natural. This can be explained with regard to the norms that are dominant in a specific domain. The most dominant norms are those that are invisible; we do not regard them as norms, we just live them. Norms about gender behaviour are among the strongest across all cultures, and visuals that are not critically looked upon or questioned contribute to the consolidation of norms, keeping them 'invisible'. Norms are also related to what we accept and agree upon as being valuable, which can be defined as *the canon* within a context (Pollock, 1999). Within the contexts of art and national art galleries, it has been a tradition to collect paintings by male artists who have been given the status of 'influential' in the context of art history. But the reason why these male artists have been influential is that they have been priced with a high value by the market (they belong to the canon) and therefore have become regarded as an economic investment for art collectors and patrons. In this context, artwork by women or people outside the Western art context have been regarded as having been less valuable. At the beginning of the 20th century, African artwork such as masks and sculptures were valued as inspiration by many early modernist artists, but they had little value as art objects in their own right. In a similar manner, textile works, mostly made by women, were not accepted as art but merely as consumer goods or handicrafts. From a larger perspective, this can be understood as being part of an ongoing struggle and negotiation of power and politics. Visuals are by no means 'innocent' observers of this, nor its institutions.

As previously mentioned, visual communication does not happen in isolation. It must be understood as a communicative act and activity. From the spectator or recipient's point of view, this act often has some kind of need as its starting point, a motivating reason to learn the meaning of a visual. For example, anyone who gets a driver's license has to learn how to read traffic signs as a part of the test. The theoretical test on the signs' meanings is one context, and the situation can be stressful since one needs to remember the meanings precisely. As soon as one gets the driver's license, one enters another context. Even though one has experienced the roads as a passenger before, the situation will change radically. One needs to pay attention to the traffic signs that provide guidance on how to drive, where to drive or not, and one must also pay attention to speed limits and much more. The point is that there are always lessons involved in visual communication. We need to develop skills to be able to interpret even the most 'ordinary' visuals around us.

In Figure 5.5, we see a picture from a street showing what a meeting between cars and bicycles is expected to look like. The simple-looking sign does not follow the pictorial language of other traffic signs. Still, its content is more complex than it first appears. What does the arrow mean? Is the car driver expected to move into the bicycle path when they meet another car? All of this needs to be interpreted in the driving situation. The sign is only of interest to drivers and those who ride bikes; not to pedestrians who can stop and reflect upon its content. However, in the driving situation, it is likely the drivers and cyclists will not have time to read the sign since they are preoccupied with the traffic situation and their respective efforts to avoid accidents.

Notations

A *notation* can be defined as a system of characters, symbols or abbreviated expressions used in art, science, mathematics or logic to express technical facts or quantities. It can also be a series of ad hoc jottings made to support memory or a discussion. A notation is thus a means of visualising and framing thoughts and ideas. The use of notations varies between subjects, but also within each subject. For example, a notation can be used as an instruction for how to perform the movements of a dance or how to play a piece of music. Using a notation, it is possible to compose and communicate music and choreograph a dance performance. But notations are also used to visualise invisible things like chemical compounds or physical phenomena such as rays of light.

For the uninitiated, even simple-looking notations are often beyond comprehension. In Noa Eshkol and Abraham Wachman's book *Movement Notation* (1958),

FIGURE 5.5   Photography: Yvonne Eriksson.

This photo shows a road sign in Stockholm that aims to instruct motorists and bicyclists how to drive when meeting on the road. However, the sign is placed so high above the road that drivers must look upward in order to read the instruction and, by that, divert their attention away from what is happening on the road.

notations for dance are presented. Even though the design of the notations is simple, their interpretation requires expertise in choreography. However, the founder of the system does not leave notations without comments. In the two pictures (Figures 5.6 and 5.7) we see how the notations are indexed with explanations. Even so, all notations are open for some kind of interpretation. In music, for example, the written musical notes have fixed meanings in the sense that they relate to certain tones, in C or G minor for instance. But in the score, there will be additional playing instructions for the interpreters of the musical piece: *piano*, *forte*, and so on.

Framing

Framing is an essential part of our understanding of visuals. It is the way in which we draw the lines around something that connects or separates the elements in a picture; influencing whether we interpret them as discrete or belonging together. This is something that was covered in Chapter 3.

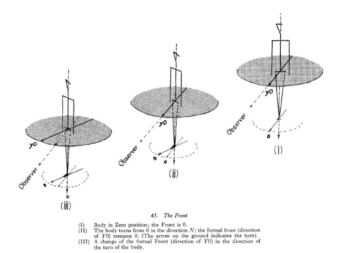

43. *The Front*

(I)   Body in Zero position; the Front is 0.
(II) The body turns from 0 in the direction *N*; the formal front (direction of *Y*0) remains 0. (The arrow on the ground indicates the turn).
(III) A change of the formal Front (direction of *Y*0) in the direction of the turn of the body.

FIGURE 5.6 Examples from *Movement Notation*, by Noa Eshkol and Abraham Wachman, 1958.

51. *The Shift of the Longitudinal Axis of the Pelvis*

52. (a) The Torso is in a Passive Position (as a result of maximal release of muscular tension).
(b) A Tilted Position of the Torso (the relation between its component parts remaining as in Zero position).

FIGURE 5.7 Examples from *Movement Notation*, by Noa Eshkol and Abraham Wachman, 1958.

Framing theory is a theoretical and analytical tool used to explain and predict visual material and its effects. It is used widely in communication studies and when analysing news media and its effects, but it has its origins in Irving Goffman's sociology (*Frame Analysis: an essay on the organisation of experience*,

1974). Goffman provides a theory of frames as 'schemata of interpretations' that allow us to make sense of events in everyday life and make meaning of 'what is going on'. In other words, we use frames to interpret the experiences we make in the present, and in doing this we have to use our previous experiences as schemata. Frames are socially shared and culture-specific, and provide contexts which enable our interpretation of events (Goffman, 1974). In his study of advertisements in magazines with a focus on gender display, *Gender advertisement* (1979), Goffman examines how femininity and masculinity are constructed and framed through a conventionalised use of certain visual tropes and signs. These can be understood as frames of ritualised female subordination, where masculinity and femininity are consistently reproduced in an unequal and hierarchical relationship. One could argue that our visual culture, and thus also our 'visual behaviour', the ways we interact with visuals, have most certainly undergone major changes since Goffman conducted his studies. Of course, this is true to a large extent. At the same time—as the basic argument in this book is that we must rely on both vision and visuality to understand how we interpret and interact with visuals—our everyday visual events have both more stable and rapidly changing characteristics.

When analysing and interpreting visuals, identifying the context is one way to 'frame' their meanings. Thus, to frame something is to both narrow down possible readings and to place focus on certain aspects of visuals. We need to take several aspects of framing into account: the aim of the visual, the context in which the visual appears and where the spectator is located or—as in the case of visuals for instruction—where the user of the visual is supposed to perform the act. Also, from the perspective of a creator or producer, framing is to be understood as formulating what is going to be visualised and how. A question that often arises in relation to context is, 'how broad should we allow the context to be?' When spectators or recipients frame what to study and interpret in a visual artefact, the frame not only holds the visual, but also carries historical and ideological implications. This is therefore an act we perform as spectators.

Thus framing can be understood as an act of meaning-making. But framing is also an act that can be performed by someone else with the aim of directing our thoughts and understandings. Moreover, as in the examples given by Theo van Leeuwen, framing is also a multimodal principle: it is not only a principle in visual composition but can also be used physically, for example, to divide space, people and actions. In other words, framing is a common semiotic principle, realised by different semiotic resources in different semiotic modes' (van Leeuwen, 2005:14). Framing between public and private spheres is a common way to physically order a space. Nowadays, so-called activity-based offices are also popular, where each room is designed in a way that indicates what kind of activity should be conducted in it. The framing is thus embedded in the space itself.

Teresa's ecstasy in context

It is not just artworks and artists that have become canonised. Certain readings and interpretations of motifs have also become more canonised than others. The interpretations we make obviously depend on the situation and context, as well as the framing. The following close reading of a piece of art from the 17th century serves as an example of the complexity involved in the way framing works.

There are many historical examples of religious and mythological themes that have led to debates on how to interpret these motifs and how they are portrayed. An interpretation is, of course, just that: a subjective reading and not an objective statement. Still, by taking different elements into consideration such as context and framing, in all their aspects— historical, architectural and visual—we can still make a plausible reading. One example is *The Ecstasy of Saint Teresa*. This is a sculptural group that is said to have provoked concern with its erotic overtones, from the very time it was finished. But what can we, from our contemporary Western viewpoint, see in a representation of the phenomenon which should express religious ecstasy—and how can we understand it?

The sculptural group represents the Spanish national saint Teresa (1515–1582), who founded the stricter branch of the Carmelite nuns in 1562 and played an important role in Catholic mysticism. The sculpture depicting Saint Teresa is part of an altar in the Cornaro Chapel in Rome made between 1645 and 1652 by Gianlorenzo Bernini (1589–1680) (Figure 5.8).

FIGURE 5.8 *Teresa's ecstasy*, Bernini, 1645–1652.

In the sculpture, Bernini has embodied Saint Teresa's vision, which she is said to have described as follows:

> I saw in his hand a long spear of gold, and at the iron's point there seemed to be a little fire. He appeared to me to be thrusting it at times into my heart, and to pierce my very entrails; when he drew it out, he seemed to draw them out also, and to leave me all on fire with a great love of God. The pain was so great, that it made me moan; and yet so surpassing was the sweetness of this excessive pain, that I could not wish to be rid of it. The soul is satisfied now with nothing less than God. The pain is not bodily, but spiritual; though the body has its share in it. It is a caressing of love so sweet which now takes place between the soul and God, that I pray God of His goodness to make him experience it who may think that I am lying.[1]

In the historical art overview work titled *A World History of Art* by Hugh Honour and John Fleming (1982), Saint Teresa's ecstasy is described as follows:

> … St. Teresa, head thrown back, mouth open and eyes closed in an attitude of physical abandon, has obvious erotic overtones and aroused adverse comments from contemporaries. But Bernini goes beyond a direct representation of her experience—so direct that her convulsive condition might almost be diagnosed by a twentieth century psychologist—to hint at the phenomenon of her levitation after receiving communion and also her miraculous transformation into a beautiful young woman at the moment of her death, so that the group becomes a richly allusive image of the state, midway between heaven and earth, when spirit and matter meet.
>
> *(Honour & Fleming, 1982: 590)*

In their interpretation of Saint Teresa's own description, the authors seek to elevate the experience from the physical to the metaphysical. If we study the sculpture of Teresa in detail, we can find other possible interpretations than the one given by Honour and Fleming. Saint Teresa sits slightly reclined upon a cloud-like formation. She rests her right foot on the cloud while her left one hangs freely in the air and points downwards. Her left arm hangs straight down while the right one is held by the angel's left hand. The angel stands facing her and looks down on her face. Saint Teresa's eyes are closed and her mouth half-open. The angel directs the spear towards Teresa's womb while he bends his arm slightly backwards. He holds the spear between his index finger and thumb while slightly bending the other fingers. This is a hand movement that has been described as obscene in visual artwork with hidden erotic symbolism (Leppert, 1996).

In the text, Teresa describes how she is pierced in the heart. However, in the sculpture, the spear is not aimed at the heart. The description of physical ecstasy that Teresa gives can also be interpreted as a symbol of a strong sexual experience: here the saint/woman allows God to penetrate her body. In the staging of the motif, Bernini also uses signs of physical female ecstasy: the female body passive with the head tilted back, closed eyes (which in itself is a symbol of passive sexuality) and a half-open mouth; available to be ingested visually and, on a symbolic level, physically. Honour and Fleming's interpretation that Bernini has depicted Teresa's moment of death 'when spirit and matter meet' does nothing to deprive the sculptural group of its expression of physical female ecstasy.

We will now move on in our analysis to examine how the external context, and the manner in which the motif is framed, contribute to making the image of ecstasy available as visual pleasure. Saint Teresa's ecstasy is performed for a funeral chapel in memory of the family of Cardinal Federico Cornaro and is flanked by two balconies which represent prayer pulpits, with male family representatives depicted in half-figure. Teresa's ecstasy is thus available not only to the viewer and visitor but also within the work in the sense that there are viewers present whose focus is on Teresa. First of all, the angel's gaze is directed towards her body, which is reinforced by the spear whose tip points towards her womb. There are also the eyes of the men seated in the balconies. Taken altogether, these elements function as focalisers and help lead the viewer's gaze towards Teresa's bodily ecstasy. Saint Teresa is thus very much framed. The figure of Teresa, the centre of the sculptural group, is framed by the flanked prayer pulpits and the contemplative gazes. But, in addition, Teresa as a representation of a woman—maybe in the form of a saint—is framed, and, in that sense, delimited.

With the help of the concept of a frame, let us look at a few more examples of how visual representations of women can function as a means of controlling and limiting the image of women and, thus, also as a means of showing how a 'woman' can be understood.

Framing the body in visual culture

In English, 'to frame' is not just about the act of placing a frame around a painting; it also carries a number of broader meanings. In all its ambiguity, the English phrase 'to frame' is a useful concept in this discussion of the (female) body in visual culture. It can mean to adapt or fit into existing frames, or to shape, but it can also mean to delimit someone or something, drawing boundaries around something—not least, around the human body. Separating the inside from the outside also has a psychological dimension; it is about drawing boundaries around one's own subjectivity, and defining and creating an individual identity. Not least, it is about our need for control, something that all demarcation and enforcement of borders expresses. This may take a number of forms: a border between nature and culture, our own and others', us and them, and so on. In art, we can identify a recurring theme which, in several ways, points to a need to control the woman and the female body. Namely, the nude study or the female nude.

In her classic text, *The female nude: Art, obscenity and sexuality* (1992), the feminist art historian Lynda Nead writes about this style of representation. She claims

that the female nude has been a central motif in Western art because representations of the female body can also be viewed as an attempt to adapt and delimit
a foreign and frightening body. This process is not least about transforming the
woman/nature into culture mastered. Exposing the female body to the practices
and conventions of art and aesthetics is a way of controlling an ungovernable
body and placing it within the 'safe boundaries' of culture. In order for us to
understand how the image of the naked woman can be seen as a transformation
from nature to culture, we can think of the distinction between being undressed
and being naked that exists in art—*naked* versus *nude*. The origins of this distinction are found in Kenneth Clark's *The Nude* from 1956 in which Clark examines one of art history's most common motifs spanning from Greek antiquity to
European modernism. In one section of the book, Clark discusses the difference
between the naked body and the nude. The naked body shows nudity that is
too attached to 'real' bodies. Here, the body appears naked in the sense that it
is unprotected, deprived of its clothes. It has nothing to do with art. The nude
body is certainly without clothes but, at the same time, it is 'dressed' in culture.
By being presented as a cultural representation, the actual body is transformed
into an ideal one. Thus, it also becomes permissible and available to enjoy as art.
It has been transformed from nature into a controlled culture.

In the sculpture, *Jannica and the doll's pram*, by Gunnel Frieberg, something
interesting happens with the concepts of nude and naked. The statue is placed
in a busy city park in Stockholm. As museum-goers or city flâneurs, we have
learned that the statues we see of females or males without clothes are supposed
to be looked upon as nudes. That is, most often they are named after gods, god-
desses, mythical geniuses and the like. In the case of this sculpture, however, we
are presented with a 'real' person, namely Jannica, who we recognise as a young
girl. She is not wearing any clothes. Her body is represented in the stage of early
puberty, with the hips and waistline of a young woman. At the same time, she
holds on to a doll's pram with one hand and, with the other, she holds a doll
to her chest. The statue of a young, naked girl in the act of playing with her
doll obviously causes disturbance among several spectators. She seems exposed,
which urges passers-by to help cover her up, to dress her. The fact that Jannica
appears as an individual makes it very hard to enjoy this sculpture as a nude. The
question of whether this was actually the artist's intention or not is, in this case,
overruled by the spectators' inclination to identify a young girl with nothing to
wear (Figures 5.9, 5.10).

Nead finds the controlling practice of turning nature into culture particularly
evident in the reshaping of the female body:

> The transformation of the female body into the female nude is thus an act
> of regulation: of the female body and of the potentially wayward viewer
> whose wandering eye is disciplined by the conventions and protocols of art.
>
> *(Nead, 1992:11)*

FIGURE 5.9 *Jannica with the doll carriage* by Gunnel Frieberg, 1986.

Photography: Anette Göthlund.

Although this regulation involves the viewer, Nead points out that one of the main purposes of the female act study has been the regulation of the female sexual body. The nude is thus a strongly regulated representation of a female body, and one of the most important parameters in this representation is the passivity of the female body. As we have seen, these boundaries, conventions and poses have taken centuries to establish in the visual culture and are therefore even visible today. The prevailing body ideal, for both men and women, is the hard body, without visible fat and with clear, sharp contours. In order for a woman to achieve this effect, greater efforts are usually required compared to men. Female shapes with a bust and round hips offer significantly more resistance when they are to be changed. In addition, pregnancy and childbirth, for example, greatly contribute to high-lighting body parts such as the thighs, buttocks, abdomen and bust. These are the body parts most women are dissatisfied with and that they find difficult to control. When we trim the body to a hard, controlled surface and regulate ourselves in style, behaviour and appearance, the act of trimming and controlling can be seen as a choice to not challenge the norm for the femininity ideal of our time.

It is interesting and important to notice the existence of resistance to these norms and regulations, so-called 'body positivism' being part of this. Actually, if

FIGURE 5.10   *Jannica with the doll carriage*, 1986. Here, someone has covered her naked body with a scarf and a piece of cloth.

Photography: Yvonne Eriksson.

one takes a closer look at art history, it is possible to identify a feminist counter-movement. It is most visible in the art of the 1970s and is still ongoing. There are many artists who have paved the way for women to perform their body positivism on the internet today. Still, these 'foremothers' are often not very well known to others apart from art historians or those interested in feminist art. More often than not, they were held outside the canon, even if many of them have seen a late revival. One can think of artists such as Hannah Wilke (1940–1993), Judy Chicago (b. 1939), Carolee Schneeman (1939–2019) or Niki de Saint Phalle (1930–2002), all of whom were part of a movement which started in the late 1960s and explored and presented alternative representations of the female body.

The need for control is thus about a cultural tendency in the footsteps of modernity, with very wide implications. As a part of visual communication, the normative urge is that it is important to maintain control over one's own person, one's own body, sexuality, the environment, career, finances, the future and so on. The demand that one can and should improve one's own body is still directed more often towards women than towards men. However, there are indications that men are experiencing the same demands to a greater extent than ever before.

The call for men to control their body and appearance has usually appeared in a limited number of special magazines that deal with specific aspects such as sports, bodybuilding and tattooing. Today, while printed media loses its grip as the foremost visual media for instructions on 'how to' get a six-pack in three months, for example, it is easy to find just as many websites, and posts on Facebook or Instagram that deal with fitness, bodybuilding, fashion, and beauty, addressing both men and women. How their content differs is a question for another study.

Framing photographs as evidence or illusion

Photography has never been a unified concept or a single practice. When we look at a photograph, it is not easy for the untrained eye to detect whether it is analogue or digital, or a 3D model that has been rendered and, by that, looks like a photograph.[2] The idea that photography is an indexical—and therefore 'true'—representation of a specific object, environment or person is something that is questioned today, since many people know through experience how relatively easy it is to change a digital photograph. There are not necessarily any fixed referents outside the photograph, which 'deepfake' videos have shown, for example.[3] While the act of faking content is not new, deepfakes leverage powerful techniques from machine learning and AI to manipulate or generate visual and audio content with a high potential to deceive. A deepfake can also be a picture of a future building or residential area made from a rendered 3D model to make it look like a photograph of something that already exists.

If we look at various discussions in both history and contemporary society, one can detect an ambivalent relationship to photographs and photography. For example, the ongoing discussion around the ability to manipulate photographs, especially digital ones. But actually, the manipulation of photographs has been an issue since the birth of the technique in the 1840s. In the early days of portrait photography, the photographer retouched details such as a person's nose, eyebrows, etcetera according to the requests of their customers. The foremost common idea behind these alterations was to highlight what was considered to be family traits (Söderlind, 1994). From early on, photography studios also hand-coloured parts of black and white photographs, such as lips and clothes, with the intention of making the image more 'real' and individualistic. In portraits of wedding couples, the flower bouquets were often hand-coloured to remind viewers of the 'real flowers'. The retoucher was either the photographer or a specialist, often a woman. It was also common to hand-colour postcards. This tradition ended in the early 1970s, when technology developed and printing colour photographs became less expensive. This kind of added information in a photograph creates a shift of meaning from the original photograph. The expression of the photograph differs depending on the skills of the retoucher. Adding a touch of chestnut brown to a braid, soft pink to the lips or green to the eyes required skilled artists, which the retouchers were sometimes called.

Manipulation, like adding or removing details in existing photographs, also has a long history. Still, with digital technology, it is harder to detect whether or not a photograph has been manipulated in that sense. Often, we are more inclined to detect manipulation in the form of a reduction of wrinkles or other age-specific traits in official pictures of celebrities or politicians. This is so common, that we automatically detect the gap between reality and representation.

In parallel with the scepticism we show in relation to photographs, we still use them as a testimony of what goes on in our daily lives and the world around us. It can be very trivial things such as a picture, maybe a selfie, showing 'I was here', that we post on social media. Photographs are also frequently used in reporting, for example in news broadcasting, newspapers or web pages as 'proof' of what is going on. We tend to ask for visible proof when something unusual, and maybe terrifying and hard to grasp, has happened. We need to frame a moment in a course of events that might be contested and questioned.

These pictures of 'truth' might be snapshots of incidents registered by passers-by or taken by professional photographers. A picture's level of authenticity or trueness is often considered to be higher if the snapshot was taken by someone from the public, like an 'innocent eye', who just happened to pass by and register, for example, a demonstration, protest or accident. Still, pictorial conventions have developed for how to represent both war photos and 'snapshots'. The history of war photography is almost as old as photography itself, and famous war photographers like Robert Capa (1913–1954) have been part of shaping the style conventions for these photographs. Most important for the snapshot is its immediate and unprepared character—which can, of course, be staged. This is something certain groups highlight during specific incidents: 'You say this is true, we say it is fake.' It looks as if we have ended up in an uncertain space where it is impossible to frame photography either as evidence or as an illusion or phantasm. And yet there are discourses where visual evidence is still called for, such as in a courtroom where forensic photographs are used to help frame 'what really happened'.

There are many contemporary artists whose work comments on this idea of photography's ability to 'be authentic' and how it is used as proof. One example is the Swedish artist and photographer Annika Elisabeth von Hausswolff (born 1967), who has shown an interest in exploring the aesthetics of crime scene photography—and connecting it with feminist ideas. She stages and leads the viewer into her violent, yet silent, crime scenes. The witness might be a dog, a witness who cannot tell, like in the acclaimed work *Hey Buster! What Do You Know About Desire?* (1995) where a German shepherd is waiting, maybe guarding, the lifeless body of a woman on a beach. Another, earlier, work is the series *Untitled (A Study in Politics)* (1993). This shows five oval close-ups of bruised, battered female body parts: necks, arms, shoulders. These photographs are 'authentic' in the sense that the artist accessed these through the National Board of Forensic Medicine.

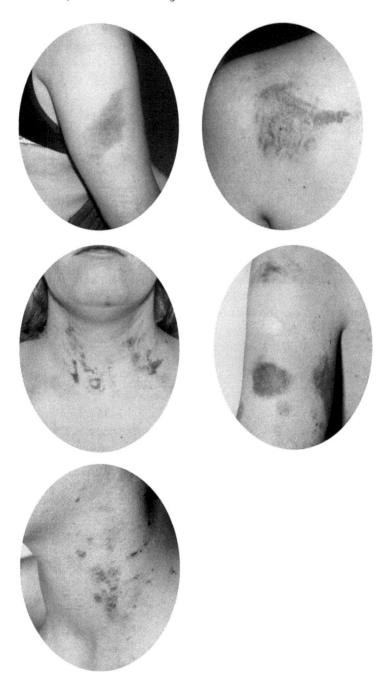

FIGURE 5.11 *Untitled. En studie politik* ('A Study in politics'), by Annika Elisabeth von Hausswolf, 1993/2020, Inkjet print.

Photo reproduction: Tomas Fischer, Moderna Museet.

The series was widely shown and, eventually, the artist felt she had lost control over the context in which the images were displayed and chose to withdraw the work. In a sense, the artwork no longer existed. However, when she was invited to have a solo show at the Moderna Museet in Stockholm in 2022, she reused the old negatives and created a new version of the work.[4] It is interesting to think about how we would react to this procedure if it was instead a painting that 'reappeared'. Are the photographs in the series *Untitled (A Study in Politics)* still 'proof' of violence against women, or have they become more of an illusion? Or maybe an illustration? (Figure 5.11).

Key chapter takeaways

- A context can be experienced differently depending on the situation which, in turn, affects how we understand visual representations and how they come into use.
- For visuals to make sense and in order for them to come into use, specific competencies are required from the viewer. This is also the case when we speak about simple visuals such as pictograms and notations.
- Framing has implications, regardless of whether we are talking about the framing of a work of art, the human body or a situation.

Notes

1 Vision of Saint Teresa, taken from Honour & Fleming 1982.
2 Rendering a still image is somewhat comparable to pulling the trigger on a camera in the real world, though in a 3D programme that process usually takes much longer than the shutter in a physical camera. The software has to process the 3D scene (shapes, materials, light) based on the angle chosen and render an image. It can take anywhere from half a minute to many hours, depending on the complexity of the scene and the resolution of the image. Still images and movies/animations can be rendered directly from the 3D software or external rendering software. Then there is real-time rendering, like in 3D games, where everything is rendered quickly while the player 'moves' in the environment. More complex process, but that's about where my knowledge ends.
3 *Deepfakes*, a term which combines the terms 'deep learning' and 'fake', are synthetic media in which a person in an existing image or video is replaced with someone else's likeness.
4 Anna Tellgren (2021). Annika Elisabeth von Hausswolff. On photography in a world of images. In *Annika Elisabeth von Hausswolff. Alternativ sekretess/Alternative Secrecy*, Moderna Museet: Verlag der Buchhandlung Walther und Franz König, Köln.

6

CHANGING TIME, PLACE AND MEDIA

In the previous chapter, we discussed how different contexts and situations impact the way we encounter and understand visuals, as well as how they influence communication. In this chapter, the investigation continues. Now, we will look at how the circumstances in which a visual appears affect its meaning and purpose from the vantage point of the visual's tendency to travel across time and space. Visuals not only travel across time and space, but also change the medium and technology through which they journey and appear. With each new appearance, a visual event is performed—yielding a visual encounter with a unique meaning.

One example from the art world is a piece of art by the British-Nigerian artist Yinka Shonibare, in which everything is dislocated in relation to time and space. Shonibare uses Ankara fabric from West Africa in several of his sculptures and installations. He identifies himself as a global citizen and his use of Ankara fabric is a way to deconstruct the idea of the fabric being African. The fabric was taken to West Africa by the Dutch in the 19th century, and they learned the printing technique from Indonesia. For installations and performances, Shonibare has designed dresses with this fabric that are typical of the French and British aristocracy from the 18th and 19th centuries. Although he works with different techniques and materials, his art includes traces and narrations that travel in time and space: alternative stories that challenge and deconstruct old narratives (yinkashonibare.com).

Another example is the fact that visuals that were once only accessible during a physical museum visit are now possible to view from one's home via a personal screen, and whenever one wants. This means that a single visual is simultaneously accessible to different people in different time zones, and in different parts of the world. When planning a visit to a museum, for instance, one can search for

DOI: 10.4324/9781003170037-7

related information and pictures on the internet. By looking at the museum or exhibition website, one can gather information about the collection or exhibition in advance. This preview influences one's expectations and in-person reception of the actual exhibition, collection or place.

In the following pages, we will revisit the idea of visual landscapes which was introduced in the first chapter. But we are also situated in geographical landscapes, in an actual place such as a specific country, city, or village, which carry different cultural connotations—and from those positions, we not only take part in information but also experience things differently based on the circumstances. For example, one can take part in an online meeting where one shares a visual space with the other participants—the screen and what is on the screen—but not the place. Afterwards, when one turns off the screen, gets up from the desk and perhaps leaves the house, one no longer shares either a space or place.

Maps and the representation of landscapes

In the late 1960s, the geographer Herbert Lehman discussed the differences between the topographical landscape and landscape paintings (Lehman, 1968). This is interesting to think about in connection to the cartographer's work and the decisions they must make regarding the representation of topography. According to Lehman, landscape paintings are based on the impressions of landscapes, while geographical representations are based on mathematical calculations. Therefore, the two forms of representation will carry different meanings. Even though there are differences between topographical landscapes and landscape paintings or photography, Lehman emphasises that a cartographer who describes a particular unknown landscape will benefit from an awareness of that landscape's cultural and historical conditions, as represented in paintings or photography. From a visual study perspective, W.J.T. Mitchell notes that the nature we refer to as 'a landscape' does not become a landscape until the spectator recognises and represents it, and thus labels it as such (Mitchell, 2002).

According to the philosopher Edward S. Casey, a representation of a landscape consists of a mixture of 'place-at' (at the place), 'place-of' (from a place) and 'place-for', which offers a third place, that is a 'place for looking' (Casey, 2005). This is also the place for what Casey labels a 'poetic truth', which is where the artist's view and the spectator's view meet in the artwork itself. These places created by artists also influence the way we look at actual landscapes. Griselda Pollock shows through her study of Vincent Van Gogh that the landscape in the south of France is not as colourful as the artist's paintings represent it to be, yet people tend to perceive the actual landscape as especially colourful when visiting the locations portrayed in his paintings (Pollock, 1978).

The relationship between landscape paintings and maps is also recognisable from early art history. The map is used as an example to describe how the concept of *visual culture* can be understood by the art historian Svetlana Alpers in a text from 1983. She used the term to describe how Dutch art of the 17th century is fundamentally different from the art of the Italian Renaissance. While Italian art is the primary expression of *textual culture*, a culture which seeks emblematic, allegorical or philosophical meanings in a painting, Dutch art arises from and enacts a truly visual culture. It represents a system of values in which meaning is not 'read' but 'seen' and, in this way, new knowledge is visually recorded (Alpers, 1983).

Maps visually communicate the cartographer's work, forming a scientific and artistic representation of a certain space. They offer a way to both understand the world and navigate and orient oneself in it. In conformity with other visual representations, maps only partly mirror an environment. Still, the map enables a mental picture of a specific area—larger or more limited. Maps are graphical representations that provide a spatial explanation of phenomena, concepts or events in the world. Reading a map is not an inherent human ability, but something we must learn. To be able to use a map of a given location, one needs to know where one is situated in relation to it. When using a map as a navigation tool, one also needs to be able to relate the map to the surrounding environment. Maps are therefore not only related to visuality and visual coding/decoding, but also to spatiality and spatial coding/decoding.

Today, we mostly use maps produced from satellite pictures which we follow on a smartphone as we navigate step by step. These representations can be more or less detailed but, due to the small screen a smartphone offers, they rarely provide an overview of larger areas. Using digital technology to navigate at sea or while driving a car has been done for quite some time. However, there is an important difference between the 'old-fashioned' physical map and the common digital Google map: the digital map is a tool for navigation and not primarily a map showing an overview and spatial relations. If one zooms out on the digital map on one's smartphone or the screen in one's car, for example, the visual representation will be on such a small scale that it will be difficult to read. This is one reason why physical maps remain in use. Still, they might not be considered as the most important travel companion. It could be argued that the combined use of the traditional map—whether it is the World Atlas or a city map—and the digital map provides the most functional way to orientate oneself in the world.

Decoding a digital map, which constantly shifts before one's eyes while one moves, requires a special kind of competence which, of course, must also be learned. In the same manner that abilities related to spatial navigation in the physical environment differ from person to person, these abilities also differ when spatial navigation is transferred to two dimensions. Sense of space is a core cognitive ability, but our brains' capacity to convert three-dimensional space into two dimensions and vice versa is, to a certain extent, individual—but most of all, it is about practice.

Mapping

Mapping is a term that has been in focus within research and artistic practice during the last decades. It was triggered by the exploration of power relationships and in relation to the colonial annexing of continents and countries. The map has been a chosen topic for many artists, as well as mapping as a practice of exploring territories and objects. The motif is used in both a playful way and as a means of critiquing established understandings of borders between countries. Borders and boundaries are in constant flux and there is nothing objective about them; maps and their borders always express values and power. Thus, maps are very rarely singular or neutral representations of geographies or the world we live in. They are political and historical documents and objects which are up for renegotiation. If one looks at examples of maps taken into artistic practice, one can see that their functions or aims are changed. Or rather, their 'hidden' or unspoken functions and aims are exposed and used for alternative purposes such as revealing the often political, economic and colonial histories behind borders. See, for example, the works of Öyvind Fahlström, Alighiero E Boetti and Mona Hatoum.[1]

Mapping as a practice also conveys the meaning of 'mapping out', as in the action of sorting, grading and categorising. The phrase 'mapping out the terrain' is about getting an overview of a given piece of land, which can be both a geographical space and a discursive place. First, one gets an overview, then one needs to create an order out of what one sees. Say, for example, one were to map out the terrain of 19th-century art. The overview would prove a crushing dominance of male, European artists who have been written into the canon of fine art due to socio-cultural ideas of what was acceptable at the time (Pollock, 1999). The categorisation of visual culture (or anything) will most certainly influence status, since categorisation is easily followed by hierarchisation. Returning to the maps of the Dutch 17th century, 'the mapping impulse', as visualised by the artists of the time, was a way of expressing power and claiming ownership over people and countries. At the same time, the maps were, of course, important tools for navigating land and sea.

Visuals as mobile objects

To speak of visual culture is also to speak of material culture. The artefacts of visual culture are also always material in some sense, such as the maps mentioned above. In the same way, the physical world manifests itself visually. The materiality of the visual object obviously affects its movements. A grand marble sculpture of Apollo is probably made with a certain place in mind and is not so easy to move, while transporting a smaller wooden figure of a Hindu goddess would be much easier. The oil painting of *The Sleeping Venus* we enjoy in a museum has probably also travelled from the location where it was originally installed—perhaps the private chambers of a nobleman. A small photo portrait of a loved one may have travelled around the world, tucked inside a wallet. The equivalent today is, of course, the digital photos many fill their mobile phones with.

If one were to come across an old, printed map today, one would most likely hang it on the wall as decoration, instead of using it for navigating. A rare print of such a map can become a collectable and cost a lot of money. Its ability to show the right way to a destination is probably not the best, but it will provide historical information such as information about city planning during the time it was made. Part of what defines a map is obviously the fact that it can be physically moved around. It is used for planning a trip, for navigating during the actual trip, and, sometimes, it is also brought back home as a souvenir from the trip—at least if it is a paper map. While a trip is being planned, the map can also serve the function of a tool—stimulating the imagination and desires regarding what to visit, or propelling one to conduct a search on travel websites or Google Earth. Brought back as a souvenir, the map can be used to show and tell stories about the trip to friends and relatives. The map and its symbols support the memory when creating the narration from the trip, and help places come back to life. As a tool for memory, the map's representations create different images in the mind compared to photographs of the same places. Its materiality can also bring forth memories, with stains and wrinkles adding to the narrative. Of course, today, the foldable paper map exists in parallel to the digital maps one may have on one's smartphone. A paper map can be viewed as advantageous considering the fact that one does not need to recharge it or have internet access in order to use it.

Now here is an important point, and something we tend to forget in this time of rapid technological development affecting the daily lives of many: the introduction of new technology does not mean that we make a clean cut of separation from what was there before. It is also a fact that the 'new' is not introduced simultaneously across the globe. Distribution is always uneven and connected to politics and economics. New media, new technology and new 'things' always exist in parallel with the 'old'. We did not get a paperless office when the personal computer was introduced. Nor did we stop reading printed books, even though we can now read or listen to them as audiobooks on digital platforms. Many of us do both. Or we switch between mediums depending on what suits us best in a given situation. It is true that most of the old analogue technology will, sooner or later, become 'extinct' since it will no longer be produced. By then, what still exists of old TVs, cameras, and telephones with wires attached to the wall will likely end up in the dump or preserved as collectors' items. Some of these retired technologies can already be found in design museums today. It is also popular with regard to the increased popularity of 'retro' design, whether it is a telephone from the early 1900s or the 1970s—but in these cases, it will have a primarily decorative function. It is not seldom that these items get labelled as 'kitsch', while the originals end up in museums.

Visuals with different purposes

Photographs showing the fashion of the season will someday become photographs showing 'fashion in history'. The visuals eventually transform from current event documents into historical documents. Documents from times gone by can have a decorative function or become historical source material. Similar to the trajectory of old, printed maps, posters for concerts, theatre performances and exhibitions with the original aim of advertising an event eventually turn up as interior decoration objects on the wall of someone's home. Information about when and where is transformed into curiosa and memorabilia. Alternatively, the old-fashioned shoots or posters might be used for cultural analyses of gender relations or political engagement among the youth; or they may function as a source of inspiration for costume designers of theatre or film productions. Actually, every piece of art or visual representation from any era, regardless of its primary function, can *also* function as a historical document. What we need are the keys to how to interpret and decode them.

With these examples, we can see that the meaning of visuals and objects can change as a result of their mobility. This can occur from several aspects at a time, depending on where the visuals appear or reappear and what use and function they are given. As discussed in Chapter 5, meaning and context cannot be separated. Anthropologist Arjun Appadurai has studied what he calls 'the social life of things' (1986) and stresses the relationship between social identities and *things*: the meanings that people attribute to objects/things is always connected to human transactions and motivations. As shown above, the way objects are used and circulated affects their value. Objects, in turn, also lend value to social relations. In our discussion, 'things' are visual objects, but the reasoning is the same as in Appadurai's examples.

Dislocated visuals

As we have seen, certain visuals may appear in different media, forms, formats and materials. Even if a visual's origin is media-specific—such as an oil painting on a canvas or a digital image in a computer game—there is nothing that prevents it from appearing in other media, forms, formats or materials. Long before the digital era, visuals had the ability to appear and reappear in different manifestations; famous artworks turning up as reproduction prints in books is an example of this. What we see today is more and faster movement and change. Consider, for example, how J.K. Rowling's wizarding world of Harry Potter left the printed pages of the books and reappeared in the form of films, posters, toys, clothing, etcetera. If one googles 'Harry Potter + shopping' an abundance of supplies appears—nothing is too small to be part of the visual world created for the Harry Potter universe. In business terms, this intermediality has been defined as *optimal distribution*, where fictional figures appear as toys, and printed on clothing and cups, and the original picture book appears as a video. It is not only a book that is launched; it is an entire concept. In Scandinavia, one can find complete environments recreated around fictional characters, such as Pippi Longstocking's house, Villa Villerkulla in Sweden and Moomin Valley in Finland.

These examples also demonstrate the close connection between visuals and commodities. Visuals as objects can easily become part of commodity culture. And commodity culture is, of course, a part of visual culture and useful for visual communication—communicating where one has travelled, who one wants to be, where one works and so forth.

It is possible to identify the ongoing merging of cultural expressions and forms as *intertextual* and *intermedial referencing*. Initially produced by companies for an audience to consume, nowadays it is also common to find that characters and stories from popular books, films etcetera are 'overtaken' and produced by the audience in the form of fan fiction or fan art, which then creates an offspring that is taken up by a production company. And so it goes on. This phenomenon has been labelled as *convergence culture* by media analyst Henry Jenkins. In *Convergence Culture: Where Old and New Media Collide* (2006) he investigates the complex relationships between top-down corporate media and bottom-up participatory culture.

Removing a visual from its original context disengages its suggested meaning and opens up a gap where new meanings can be produced. This is what happens in fan fiction and fan art when well-known characters from the Star Wars universe, for example, are re-modelled and re-used in new and alternative narratives created by fans. Another example can be found in religious items and symbols that are taken out of their original cultural and geographical contexts. The Namji doll from Cameroon discussed in Chapter 1 is an example of this, when it is brought into a home setting on the other side of the globe and given a merely decorative function. Another example is the religious meaning of the Christian cross, which has been hijacked several times by popular culture. For instance, during the 1980s, it became one of the most frequently used decorative elements in subculture and fashion, appearing alongside other accessories worn by punk rockers, such as safety pins. Thereby, it created a bricolage signifying contempt for the bourgeois lifestyle. The cross has also been used in black metal music as a form of provocation, or by pop stars like Madonna who used it in her 'Like a Virgin' music video (1984) as a subversive feminist symbol.

Museum gaze

In a sense, most of the visual and material artefacts displayed in museums and art galleries around the world have—through their physical displacement—been subject to altered or lost meaning content. Within the field of Museology, the term 'critical' has been added, changing the name to Critical Museology; this is much like what has happened in the fields of Visual Culture Studies and Material

Culture Studies. When taking a historical and critical approach to museums' common practice of procuring, collecting, categorising and displaying artefacts, it becomes obvious that the societal role of the museum must be reassessed. Today, it is an ongoing and often lively debate that also raises questions about colonialism and power (Vergo, 1989; Lorente, 2022).

Most of us have been trained to apply a 'museum gaze' when looking at and consuming what is on display at a museum. Moreover, we have also learned how to behave inside a museum, including how to position ourselves to be educated by famous explorers, scientists and historians. The order of what is revealed to us as visitors is an important element in the museum discourse and affects our understanding of it. The hierarchies are often strict and can also be seen, for example, in the placement of certain items with high status—such as crown jewels or famous paintings—alongside items that could be considered as 'minor art' in comparison, such as handcrafted brooches or silverware. This is one example of how 'the ordering of things' affects our reading of them. Since we look for similarities, we tend to cluster things that seem appropriate together, arranging them into categories, for example; although such categories are always constructions and can be arranged in another way to tell a different story.

Pictures as consumer goods—examples from a study

It is both relevant and interesting to study the vernacular, everyday use of visual objects, including their social lives and the meanings which are collectively produced by the visuals themselves, the contexts and the spectators. In the early 2000s, an ethnographic study of media and consumer encounters in a Swedish shopping mall was conducted.[2] The aim was to study the very context in which the meeting takes place; examining the processes of consumption, communication and media use in direct relation to each other. Instead of criticising, by default, the consumption culture for seducing passive consumers, the project explored the meaning that exists and is created in what can sometimes look like irrational choices, unplanned shopping and financial waste. One location chosen for this study was a shop which sold pictures of many kinds: posters, postcards and greeting cards of any kind imaginable, as well as (relatively) more expensive reproductions on canvas. The store also had an in-store framing facility. Over the course of the study, a series interviews and observations were conducted.

The level of commitment most people showed while making their selections of both cards and pictures was striking. Of course, there were those who shopped spontaneously; mostly when it came to cards, but also in respect of the cheaper, small-sized pictures. Still, many people visited the shop several times prior to making a purchase in order to orientate themselves, and they chose items carefully whether they were to be gifts or for personal use. For many shoppers interviewed, giving paintings as gifts is considered to be a difficult but significant task. A picture is full of meaning and the idea is well established that it says something about both the recipient and the giver: the better one knows a person, the more meaningful the message and the more time is needed for reflection before the purchase. Greeting cards are, by their very nature, something one gives away, and many buyers also choose motifs and texts with great care. In the study, people tended to choose more personal and more expensive cards for recipients with whom they had a special relationship.

One of the basic ideas of the study is the same as the one advocated in this book: consumption is also communication, whether it is 'just' a greeting card, a reproduction that will hang on the living room wall or a fan poster in a teenager's room. In the interviews, it became clear that the pictures and cards—in all their varieties —had surprisingly long lifespans. It was obvious that people had a hard time letting go of something later, even if the monetary investment was small. These objects were clearly strongly connected with emotions and memories. An old theatre poster could be taken down from the kitchen wall, but not thrown away. More likely, it ended up in storage. All in all, the study of this kind of visual event, centred around the intention of purchasing a picture, was, in many ways, a confirmation that people are well aware of the communicative aspects of visuals, as well as of their importance for keeping memories alive, and the effect they have on emotions. In this case, 'authenticity' was of lesser importance.

The shop in the study, like others of its kind, was present in almost every mall around the country until recently, when the company went online. Today, when we produce so many of our own 'postcards' digitally and send them as messages on our mobile phones or computers—maybe even printing out our favourite photos at home—the store mentioned above and other stores like it are much rarer to find as physical stores. They are now replaced by online shops. However, it is still popular to buy these kinds of decorative posters in museum shops and stores with furniture and home decorations.

Souvenirs

Ever since the possibility to reproduce pictures arose—with the invention of the printing press, the birth of the photograph and, eventually, the development of mechanical reproduction—there has been a discussion about aspects of images such as originality, aura, and authenticity.[3] Especially in relation to fine art, the idea of the 'one-and-only' has not totally had its day yet since, when standing in front of a certain piece of art, we still tend to ask, 'Is it an original?' Interestingly enough, there is one visual object where the question of originality is irrelevant: Souvenirs. The word souvenir means 'memory' in French. To keep one's memories alive, a souvenir helps to make them more visible or give them a physical form.

Souvenirs of all kinds often bear the images of famous artwork, well-known landmarks, characters from popular culture and the like. The water lilies from Monet's paintings have long since left their original place in the paintings to be transformed into a printed pattern that can be seen on almost any kind of artefact—from tea mugs to bookmarks and scarves. Since there are approximately 250 different paintings by Monet of water lilies, many of them quite large, each print also reproduces only a very small part of the original painting.

When considering the fact that certain famous artworks and motifs are reproduced and appear in other contexts and media, one interesting aspect is how their meaning changes with the change of material. A piece of art is not only a motif, but its expression is also highly dependent on the art piece's materiality. Consider, for example, a painting by van Gogh, which is recognised for, among other characteristics, the brushstrokes, the sensory effect created by the way in which the oil paint was applied to the canvas, and the brightness of its colours. All of these qualities are lost when the image of the sunflowers is transferred onto elasticated cotton socks or t-shirts. One could even say the materiality of this artwork becomes diluted through these kinds of reproductions. If one has only ever encountered a motif in reproductions, one will probably be struck by the beauty of the original if one eventually comes to see it. And upon encountering the original, one may, as a consequence, end up buying a reproduction from the museum shop in order to keep that memory alive.

How it is decided which artwork becomes multiplied and spread worldwide—not least through souvenirs and tourism—is an interesting question. How does it happen that a certain piece of art is rendered such an iconic status that it gets chosen to represent an entire museum? For example, it might be the Uffizi Gallery Florence, where Sandro Botticelli's *The Birth of Venus* (1480s) is used to promote the museum's treasures, or the omnipresent meeting hands from Michelangelo's *The Creation of Adam*, which we have already considered in Chapter 2. What is obvious is that those who decide what to put on display tend to choose art that is already canonised, which means the ongoing reproduction of the canon is reinforced. Through this, we notice how the exclusion of female artists, or artists from non-Western countries, continues. One effect of this is the reproduction of a Western art canon that travels around the world.

The tote bag as a sign

Disengaged from its geographical, as well as its cultural and historical origin, the meaning of a piece of art is open for renegotiation every time it appears in a new context, such as on t-shirts, umbrellas and tote bags. The tote bag is an interesting item: a tote bag is simply a large bag suitable for carrying (or toting) lots of stuff. It can be seen hanging from the shoulder of both young and old alike. It is practical in many ways and often relatively cheap, at least if one purchases it in a material like a textile. Of course, not everyone who carries around a tote bag takes notice of the visual or textual message which has become part of its visual expression. Still, it has become an item that is used for visual communication about aspects of personal, social and cultural identity, as well as about political or ideological preferences and so on. In this case, it is, of course, crucial that whoever sees an image printed on the tote bag is able to recognise and decode its message as it is carried around. Otherwise, it is merely a pattern of some kind. In other words, the visual competence of the spectator will influence the meaning of the message. A tote bag from TATE Modern in London might only have 'T-A-T-E' printed in white letters against black fabric, but it will still signal both a degree of cultural and economic status if it is carried about Stockholm, Sweden, for example (Figure 6.1). It shows that the person bearing it has the economic means to travel to the UK, as well as an interest in contemporary art. If, instead of letters, the bag is covered with colourful, abstract patterns in black, red, blue, green and yellow, an art connoisseur with a trained eye will likely recognise the visual language of Juan Miró. This will add to the tote bag's significance as a meaning-maker and a piece of visual communication (Figure 6.1).

The same holds true for a lot of the merchandise produced for rock bands and other touring musical acts. The Iron Maiden t-shirt, showing the iconic long-haired skeleton ('Eddie') with the added text 'Killers', for example, will speak to

FIGURE 6.1 Tote bag from Tate Modern featuring a print by Joan Miró, *La Révell au Petit Jour* ('Awakening in the Early Morning') from 27 January 1941.

Photography: Hans Henningsson.

FIGURE 6.2 Iron Maiden t-shirt from the Killer 1981 world tour.

Photography: Magnus Göthlund.

dedicated fans about the Killer 1981 world tour during the heyday of the heavy metal rock band (Figure 6.2).

The date also adds the presence of time, a 'when', communicating that, 'I was there'. It is also possible that a 1981 Iron Maiden t-shirt has been purchased on eBay for a much higher price than it originally cost—signaling its owner's even more serious dedication to heavy metal subculture. What is approved and valued by some may also be detested and rejected by others. To an outsider, the old, well-worn Iron Maiden t-shirt might, of course, be nothing more than a sign of bad taste in clothing.

Visual communication, as in the examples given, is highly dependent on the ability of both the carrier of the message and the recipient of it to recognise the symbols and the exclusiveness of what could otherwise appear to be ordinary. Without such recognition, the t-shirt or tote bag might as well be one of the many mass-produced items by a big fashion retailer.

Of course, status is also something that is always being negotiated. Adorning one's living room wall with art posters featuring motifs by van Gogh, Monet or Picasso may be considered, by some, to be kitsch. This may particularly be the case if the poster in question is not an 'original' from a museum or art gallery, but instead a printed reproduction from a nondescript store. The canonised and highly valuable art piece is thus demystified and turned into a cheap commodity. Nevertheless, the poster of Monet's garden holds another kind of value for its owner; for recollective, emotional or purely aesthetic reasons.

Key chapter takeaways

- Visuals are not fixed in relation to meaning because they travel constantly in place, time and media.
- Maps are a part of visual communication.
- Our relationship with visuals is not fixed. We change our perception of, and relationship with, visuals depending on how, when and where we encounter them.
- Visual communication can work as an expression of identity which enables one to express not only group identity but also status.

Notes

1 As an introduction to the relation between art and mapping, see for example Ruth Watson, Mapping and contemporary art. *The Cartographic Journal*, vol. 46, no. 4, 2009, pp. 293–307. See also Katharine A. Harmon A. and Gayle Clemans (2010[2009]). *Map as Art: Contemporary Artists Explore Cartography*. New York: Princeton Architectural Press.

2 The study was part of a larger project called 'Popular Passages: Media in Modern Spaces of Consumption', conducted in a Stockholm suburban shopping mall, between 1998 and 2002. Anette Göthlund (2002), Posters and cards: visual genres in use. In Karin Becker, Erling Bjurström, Johan Fornäs and Hillevi Ganetz (eds.), *Men and Media in Spaces of Consumption*. Nora: Nya Doxa.

3 Walter Benjamin's famous essay 'The Work of Art in the Age of Mechanical Reproduction' was first published in German in 1935. It has been reprinted in several editions, for example in Benjamin, W. & Arendt, H. (1969). *Illuminations*. New York: Schocken Books.

REFERENCES

Alpers, S. (1983). *The Art of Describing: Dutch Art in the Seventeenth Century*. Chicago: University of Chicago Press.

Ang, I. (1985). *Watching Dallas: Soap Opera and the Melodramatic Imagination*. London: Methuen.

Appadurai, A. (Ed.) (1986). *The Social Life of Things: Commodities in Cultural Perspective*. Cambridge: Cambridge University Press.

Armstrong, R.D. (1978). *A Theory of Universals*. Cambridge: Cambridge University Press.

Arnheim, R. (1969). *Visual Thinking*. Berkeley, CA: University of California Press.

Austin, J.L. (1962). *How to Do Things with Word*. Oxford: Oxford University Press.

Baddeley, A. (2003). Working memory: looking back and looking forward. *Nature Reviews Neuroscience*, 4(x), 829–830.

Bal, M. (1985). *Narratology: Introduction to the Theory of Narrative*. Toronto: University of Toronto Press.

Barad, K.M. (2007). *Meeting the Universe Halfway: Quantum Physics and the Entanglement of Matter and Meaning*. Durham, NC: Duke University Press.

Barthes, R. (1972). *Mythologies*. London: Cape.

Barthes, R. (1977[1964]). Rhetoric of the image. Essays selected and translated by Stephen Heath. In: *Image, Music, Text*. London: Flamingo.

Barthes, R. (1981). *Camera Lucida: Reflection on Photography*. New York: Hill and Wang.

Bates, M.J. (2016). Fundamental forms of information. *Journal of American Society for Information and Technology*, 57(8), 1033–1045.

Belting, H. (2005). Image, medium body: anew approach to iconology. *Critical Inquiry*, 31(2), 302–319.

Benjamin, W. & Arendt, H. (1969). *Illuminations*. New York: Schocken Books.

Bredekamp, H. (2014). The picture act: tradition, horizon, philosophy. In: S. Marienberg, & J. Trabant (Eds.), *Bildakt at the Warburg Institute*. Berlin: De Gruyter, 3–32.

Bredekamp, H. (2018). *Image Acts: ASystematic Approach to Visual Agency*. Berlin: de Gruyter.

Brown, H.T. (1995[1896]). *Five Hundred and Seven Mechanical Movements, Embracing All Those Which Are Most Important in Dynamics, Hydraulics, Hydrostatics, Pneumatics, Steam Engines, Mill and Other Gearing, Presses, Horology, and Miscellaneous Machinery, and Including: Many Movements Never before Published and Several Which Have Only Recently Come into Use.* (Paperback ed). Mendham, NJ: Astragal Press.

Butler, J. (1990). *Gender Trouble: Feminism and the Subversion of Identity.* New York: Routledge.

Casey, E.S. (2005). *Earth-Mapping: Artists Reshaping Landscape.* Minneapolis, MN: University of Minnesota Press.

Clark, K. (1956). *The Nude: A Study of Ideal Art.* London: John Murray.

Cohen-Almagor, R. (2013). Internet history. In: R. Luppicini (Ed.), *Moral, Ethical, and Social Dilemmas in the Age of Technology: Theories and Practice.* Hershey, PA: IGI Global Publisher.

Comenius, J.A. & Hoole, C. (1664). *Joh. Amos Comnienii Orbis sensualium pictus hoc est, omnium fundamentalium in mundo rerum, & in vita actionum, pictura & nomenclatura = Joh. Amos Commenius's Visible World, or, A Picture and Nomenclature of All the Chief Things That Are in the World, and of Mens Employments Therein.* London: Printed for J. Kirton.

Cope, B. & Kalantzis, M. (Eds.) (2000). *Multiliteracies: Literacy Learning and the Design of Social Futures.* London: Routledge.

Corrigan, T. (2016). Still speed: cinematic acceleration, value, and execution. *Cinema Journal,* 55(2), 119–125.

Costello, M. (2014). Situatedness. In: T. Teo (Ed.), *Encyclopedia of Critical Psychology.* New York: Springer, 1757–1762.

Danto, A.C. (1999). *The Body/Body Problem: Selected Essays.* Berkeley, CA: University of California Press.

Doley, J. & O'Riordan, K. (2002). Virtually visible: Female cyberbodies and the medical imagination. In: A. Booth & M. Flanagan (Eds.), *Reload: Rethinking Women + Cyberculture.* London: MIT Press.

Duncum, P. (2004). Visual culture isn't just visual: multi-literacies, multimodality and meaning. *Studies in Art Education,* 45, 252–264. DOI: 10.1080/00393541.2004.11651771

Encyclopédie; ou Dictionnaire raisonné des sciences, des arts et des métiers, par une société de gens de lettres. Mis en ordre & publié par m. Diderot … & quant à la partie mathématique, par m. d'Alembert … (1751–1765). Paris: Briasson [etc.].

Eriksson, Y. (1998). *Tactile Pictures: Pictorial Representations for the Blind 1784–1940.* Acta Universitatis Gothoburgensis. Gothenburg Studies in Art and Architecture nr 4.

Eriksson, Y. (2010). *Att teckna ett liv: om Vera Nilssons konstnärskap (To Draw a Life: About the Artist Vera Nilsson).* Stockholm: Atlantis.

Eriksson, Y. & Florin, U. (2011). The relationship between a model and a full-size object or building: the perception and interpretation of models, DS 68-7: *Proceedings of the 18th International Conference of Engineering Design (ICED11).*

Eriksson, Y. & Göthlund, A. (2004/2012). *Möten med bilder. Att tolka visuella uttryck. (Encountering Pictures: Analysing Visuals)* (2nd ed.). Lund: Studentlitteratur.

Eriksson, Y. (2017). *Bildens tysta budskap. Interaktion mellan bild och text (The Silent Messages of Visuals: The Interaction between Pictures and Text).* Lund: Studentlitteratur.

Eriksson, Y. & Fundin, A. (2018). Visual management for a dynamic change. *Journal of Organizational Change Management,* 31(3), s. 712–727

Eriksson, Y., Sjölinder, M., Wallberg, A. & Söderberg, J. (2020). VR for assembly tasks in the manufacturing industry - interaction and behaviour. In: *Proceedings of the Design*

Society: Design Conference. Paper presented at 16th International Design Conference, Design 2020, 26 October 2020 through 29 October 2020. Cambridge University Press, 1697–1706.

Eriksson, Y. & Carlsson, A.-L. (2022). The challenge of designing meaningful information. In: Yvonne Eriksson (Ed.), *Different Perspectives in Design Thinking*. Boca Raton, FL: CRC Press.

Eshkol, N. & Wachman, A. (1958). *Movement Motation*. London: Weidenfeld and Nicolson.

Ferguson, E.S. (1992). *Engineering and the Mind's Eye*. Cambridge, MA: MIT Press.

Fludernik, M. (1996). *Towards a 'Natural' Narratology*. London: Routledge.

Fludernik, M. (2003). *The Fictions of Language and the Languages of Fiction: The Linguistic Representation of Speech and Consciousness*. London: Routledge.

Foster, H. (Ed.) (1988). *Vision and Visuality*. Seattle, WA: Bay Press.

Gibson, J.J. (1950). *The Perception of the Visual World*. Boston, MA: Houghton Mifflin.

Gibson, J.J. (1979). *The Ecological Approach to Visual Perception*. Boston, MA: Houghton Mifflin.

Giddens, A. (1991). *Modernity and Self-Identity: Self and Society in the Late Modern Age*. Cambridge: Polity press.

Gienow-Hecht, J. (2019). Nation branding: a useful category for international history. *Diplomacy & Statecraft*, 30(4), 755–779. DOI: 10.1080/09592296.2019.1671000

Goffman, E. (1959). *The Presentation of Self in Everyday Life*. New York: Doubleday.

Goffman, E. (1974). *Frame Analysis: An Essay on the Organization of Experience*. Cambridge, MA: Harvard University Press.

Goffman, E. (1979). *Gender Advertisement*. Cambridge, MA: Harvard University Press.

Goldschmidt, G. (1992). Serial sketching: visual problem solving in design. *Creativity Research Journal*, 23(2), 191–219. DOI:10.1080/01969729208927457

Gombrich, E.H. (1960). *Art and Illusion: A Study in the Psychology of Pictorial Representation*. London: Phaidon Press.

Grau, O. (2003). *Visual Art: From Illusion to Immersion*. Cambridge, MA: MIT Press.

Göthlund, A. (1997). *Bilder av tonårsflickor: om estetik och identitetsarbete*. Diss. Linköping: Univ. Linköping.

Göthlund, A. (2002). Posters and cards: visual genres in use. In: K. Becker, E. Bjurström, J. Fornäs, & H. Ganetz (Eds.), *Men and Media in Spaces of Consumption*. Nora: Nya Doxa.

Hall, S. (1980). Encoding/decoding. In Centre for Contemporary Cultural Studies (Ed.), *Media, Language: Working Papers in Cultural Studies*. London: Hutchinson, 128–138.

Hall, S. (Ed.) (1997). *Representation: Cultural Representations and Signifying Practices*. London: Sage.

Harmon, K.A. & Clemans, G. (2010[2009]). *Map as Art: Contemporary Artists Explore Cartography*. New York: Princeton Architectural Press.

Harris, J. (2001). *The New Art History: A Critical Introduction*. London: Routledge.

Hochberg, J. (1962). Pictorial recognition as an unlearned ability: a study of one child's performance. *The American Journal of Psychology*, 75, 4, 624–628.

Hodge, B. & Kress, G.R. (1988). *Social Semiotics*. Ithaca, NY: Cornell University Press.

Honour, H. & Fleming, J. (1982). *A World History of Art*. London: Macmillan.

Hunter, W. (1774). *Anatomia Uteri Humani Gravidi Tabulis Illustrata*. Birminghamiae: Excudebat Joannes Baskerville; MDCCLXXVV.

Jay, M. (1993). *Downcast Eye: The Denigration of Vision in Twentieth Century French Thought*. Berkeley, CA: University of California Press.

Jenkins, H. (2006). *Convergence Culture: Where Old and New Media Collide*. New York: New York University Press.

Kjørup, S. (1974). Doing things with pictures. *The Monist*, 58(2), 216–235.

Kjørup, S. (1978). Pictorial speech acts. *Erkenntnis*, 12(1), 55–71. Band: *Nummer*, 12(1), S. 55–71.

Koffka, K. (1935). *Principles of Gestalt Psychology*. London: Kegan Paul, Trench Truber & Co.

Kress, G.R. & Van Leeuwen, T. (2006). *Reading Images: The Grammar of Visual Design*. (2nd ed.) London: Routledge.

Krippendorff, K. (2006). *The Semantic Turn: ANew Foundation for Design*. Boca Raton, FL: CRC.

Köhler, W. (1970 [1947]). *Gestalt Psychology: An Introduction to New Concepts in Modern Psychology*. New York: Liveright.

Langer, S.K. (1951). *Philosophy in a New Key*. Cambridge, MA: Harvard University Press.

Lehman, H. (1968). *Formen lantschaftlicher Raumerfahrung im Spiegel der bildende Kunst*. Erlangen: Geographische Arbeiten Heft 22.

Leppert, R. (1996). *Art and the Committed Eye: The Cultural Functions of Imagery*. Boulder, CO: Westview Press.

Lorente, J.P. (2022). *Reflections on Critical Museology: Inside and Outside Museums*. Abingdon: Routledge.

Lynch, K. (1960). *The Image of the City*. Cambridge, MA: MIT Press.

McRobbie, A. (2000[1991]). *Feminism and Youth Culture*. (2nd ed.) Basingstoke: Macmillan.

Mirzoeff. (1995). *Silent Poetry: Deafness, Sign and Visual Culture in Modern France*. Princeton, N.J.: Legacy Library

Mirzoeff, N. (1999). *An Introduction to Visual Culture*. London: Routledge.

Mirzoeff, N. (Ed.) (2013). *The Visual Culture Reader*. (3rd rev. ed.). London: Routledge.

Mirzoeff, N. (2015). *How to See the World*. London: Pelican.

Mitchell, W.J.T. (1994). *Picture Theory*. Chicago: University of Chicago Press.

Mitchell, W.J.T. (Ed.) (2002). *Landscape and Power* (2nd ed.). Chicago: University of Chicago Press.

Mitchell, W.J.T. (2005). *What Do Pictures Want: The Lives and Loves of Images*. Chicago: University of Chicago Press.

Mitchell, W.J.T. (2015). *Image Science: Iconology, Visual Culture, and Media Aesthetics*. Chicago: The University of Chicago Press.

Nead, L. (1992). *The Female Nude: Art, Obscenity and Sexuality*. London: Routledge.

Nochlin, L. (1971). *Realism*. Harmondsworth: Penguin.

Pollock, G. (1999). *Differencing the Canon: Feminist Desire and the Writing of Art's Histories*. London: Routledge.

Pollock, G. (1978). *Vincent van Gogh: Artist of His Time*. London: Phaidon.

Radway, J.A. (1984/1991). *Reading the Romance: Women, Patriarchy, and Popular Literature*. Chapel Hill: University of North Carolina Press.

Rorty, R. (Ed.) (1967). *The Linguistic Turn: Recent Essays in Philosophical Method*. Chicago: University of Chicago Press.

Rose, G. (2016). *Visual Methodologies: An Introduction to Researching with Visual Materials* (4th ed.). London: Sage.

Rubin, E. (1915). *Synsoplevede Figurer*. Copenhagen: Gyldendal.

Sandström, S. (1995). *Intuition och åskådlighet*. Stockholm: Carlsson Bokförlag.

Shannon, C.E. & Weaver, W. (1949). *A mathematical theory of communication*.University of Illinois Press.

Shapiro, M. (1996). *Words and Pictures: On the Literal and the Symbolic in the Illustration of a Text*. The Hauge: Mouton.

Smith, A.C.T. & Stewart, B. (2011). Organizational rituals: features, functions and mechanisms. *International Journal of Management Reviews*, 13(2), 113–133, June 2011. DOI: 10.1111/j.1468-2370.2010.00288.x

Söderlind, S. (1994). *Porträttbruk i Sverige: 1840–1865: en funktions- och interaktionsstudie*. Diss. Linköping: University of Linköping; Stockholm: Carlsson.

Solso, R. (1994). *Cognition and the Visual Art*. Cambridge, MA: MIT Press.

Sturken, M. & Carthwright, L. (2002). *Practices of Looking: An Introduction to Visual Culture*. Oxford University Press.

Tellgren, A. (2021). Annika Elisabeth von Hausswolff. On photography in a world of images. In: *Annika Elisabeth von Hausswolff. Alternativ Sekretess/Alternative Secrecy*. Moderna Museet: Verlag der Buchhandlung Walther und Franz König, Köln.

Tversky, B. (2011). Visualizations of thought. *Topics in Cognitive Science*, 3, 499–535.

Tversky, B. (2019). *Mind in Motion, How Action Shapes Thought*. New York: Basic Books.

UNESCO. (n.d.). www.unesco.org/en/literacy

Van Leeuwen, T. (2005). *Introducing Social Semiotics*. London: Routledge.

Vergo, P. (1989). *The New Museology*. London: Reaktion.

Virilio, P. (2012). *Great Accelerator*. Cambridge: Polity Press.

Wagner, K. (2011). Moblogging, remediation and the new vernacular. *Photographies*, 4(2): 209–228.

Ware, C. (2012). *Visual Thinking for Design*. Burlington: Moran and Kaufman.

Watson, R. (2009). Mapping and contemporary art. *The Cartographic Journal*, 46(4), 293–307.

Wertheimer, M. (1923). Untersuchungen zur Lehre von der Gestalt II. *Psycologische Forschung*, 4, 301–350.

Wlazlak, P., Eriksson, Y., Johansson, G. & Ahlin, P. (2019). Visual representation for communication in geographically distributed new product development project. *Journal of Engineering Design*, 30(8/9), s. 385–403.

Zack, J. & Tversky, B. (1999). Bars and lines: astudy of graphic communication. *Memory & Cognition*, 27, 1073–1079.

INDEX

Pages in *italics* refer figures and pages followed by n refer notes.